LIVING WITH SCARVES

By

Lorraine E. Hammett

To My Daughters,

Cindy and Valerie, who both enjoy

Living With Scarves.

HISTORY OF THE KNAUGHTY LOOK

As this is being written (early 1989) my first book, "THE KNAUGHTY LOOK—THE MAGIC OF SCARF FASHION" has sold almost one million copies. Our success began in 1984 when our book became available in Canada's major department and leading fashion accessory stores.

In 1985 a selection of Canadian made scarf clips was added to the existing Knaughty Look line. And in 1986, an expanded selection of European scarf clips was made available.

The "MAGIC OF SCARF FASHION" has been distributed in the United States since the Fall of 1985. In 1987 a successful test market was conducted in Australia with distribution set up in the Spring of 1988.

The Knaughty Look team has made many television and personal appearances in both Canada and the United States.

Our team of "Knaughty Ladies", all qualified scarf consultants, is a familiar sight in the fashion accessory areas of many department stores from coast-to-coast in Canada.

Because of the enthusiasm generated by my first book, I was compelled to respond with this new edition, and offer an "Advanced Course" in scarf tying. We wanted to answer questions from women who had used "The Knaughty Look". When is a scarf appropriate and what kinds of scarves should be worn with various necklines? Which fabrics work best and what size scarf should I buy first? There were hundreds of enquiries.

Through our demonstrations, scarf clinics and feedback from our readers we learned more ways to tie scarves. We revised our book every year. But we needed more. So this year we give you "LIVING WITH SCARVES".

"LIVING WITH SCARVES" suggests the shapes and types of scarves to wear with coats, suits, jackets, dresses and sportswear. It addresses itself to various types of necklines and recommends scarf designs that compliment them. In addition, it offers more with larger scarves, shawls and oversized oblongs.

Women of all ages are now developing their skills in the art of scarf tying and enjoying their scarves every day. The scarf has become a most important fashion item, as essential an accessory as jewellry and shoes. (And we feel as important to dressing as your lingerie and pantyhose!)

"LIVING WITH SCARVES" offers the best of "THE KNAUGHTY LOOK" along with fashion ideas with accents, scarf clips and other dynamic new ways of wearing your scarves. We've worked hard to give you the best designs with precise, easy to follow instructions and diagrams. We're very excited about our new techniques and ideas. Scarf fashion is evolving and we're thrilled to be part of it.

So have fun learning the "how to" lesson, let your wishful thoughts become reality as you master each and every one of these sensational scarf looks in "LIVING WITH SCARVES". Let us know how you like the book, or if you've any questions. And let's start "LIVING WITH SCARVES"!

TABLE OF CONTENTS

TABLE OF CONTENTS

NECKLINES

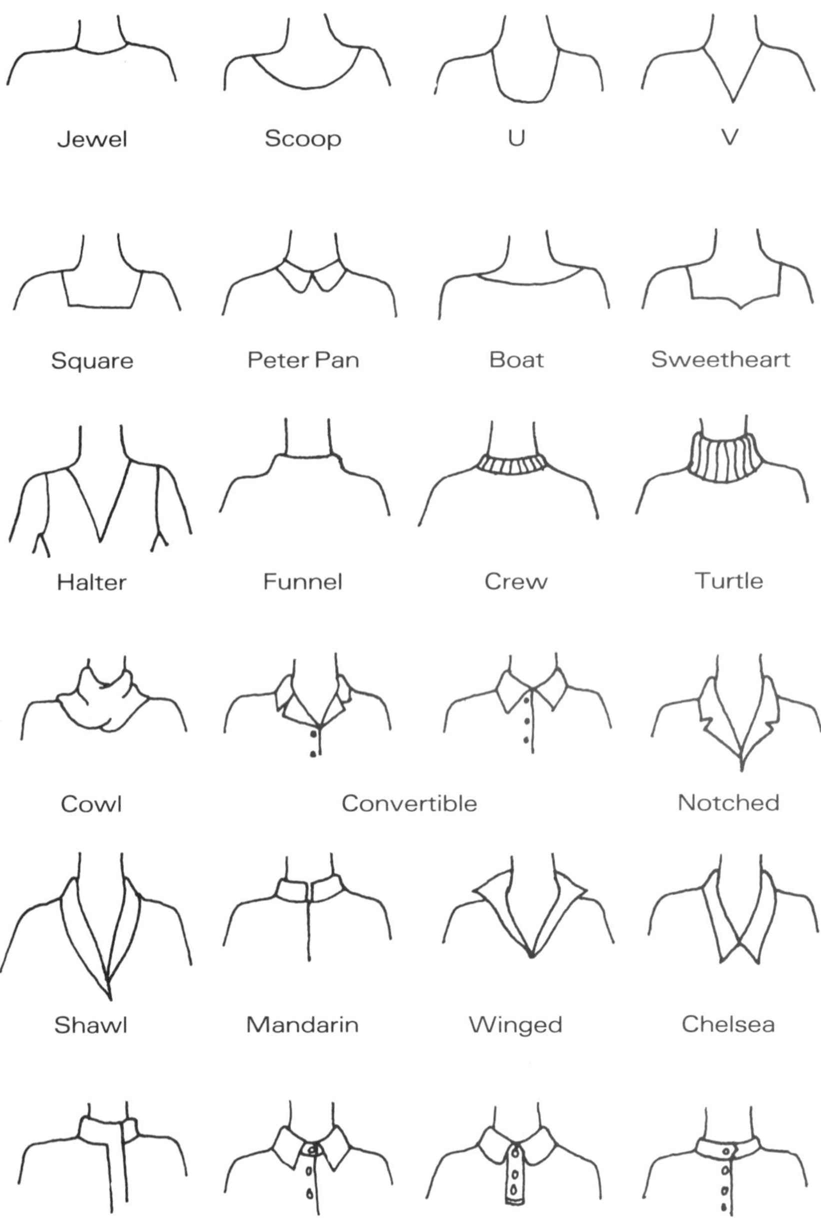
Jewel
Scoop
U
V
Square
Peter Pan
Boat
Sweetheart
Halter
Funnel
Crew
Turtle
Cowl
Convertible
Notched
Shawl
Mandarin
Winged
Chelsea
Cossack
Tailored Shirt
Polo/Golf
Collar Band

NECK LENGTHS

Short Necks — Think Vertical

Short necks need the illusion of length. Oblong scarves worn open around your shoulders will draw the eyes down. Short hair, simple jewellery and a scarf well placed will elongate the neck and face. Wear neck lines with deep V openings or with low collars.

Long Necks — Think Horizontal

Long necks can look shorter with a little art. Shoulder length hair styles are best, especially with soft waves that fall around your ears and neck. Avoid straight, severe hairdos. Try a cowl or turtle neck with scarves worn across the neck and shoulders.

While working with Living With Scarves, you will find a scarf design with a specific neckline. As you develop your skills and interest in scarves, experiment and try the designs with other necklines and apparel.

HELPFUL HINTS FOR SUCCESSFUL RESULTS

BASIC SCARF FOLDING

A Square Into A Bias

A Square Into An Oblong

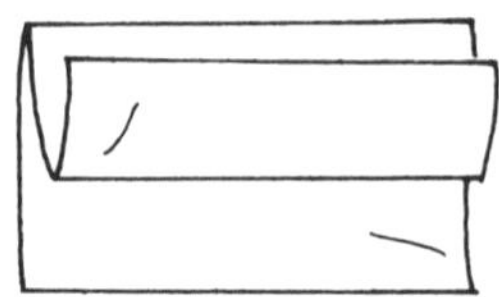

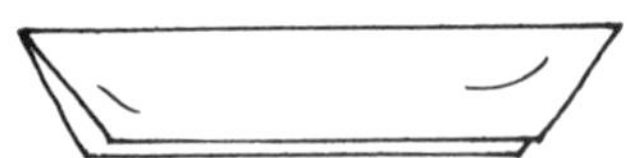

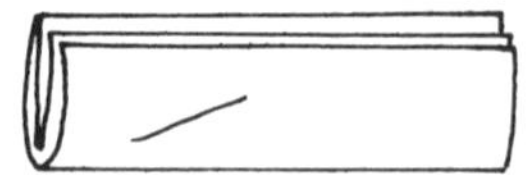

Square Knot

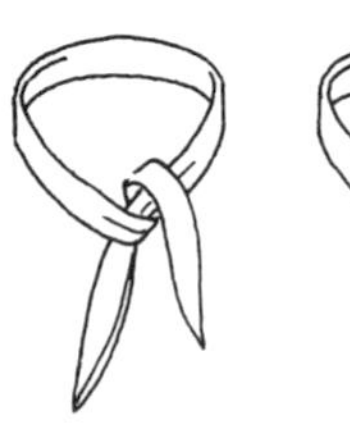

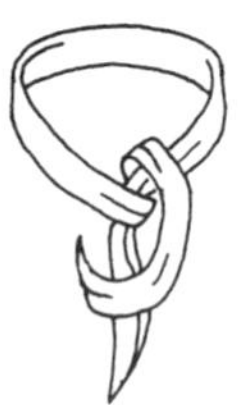

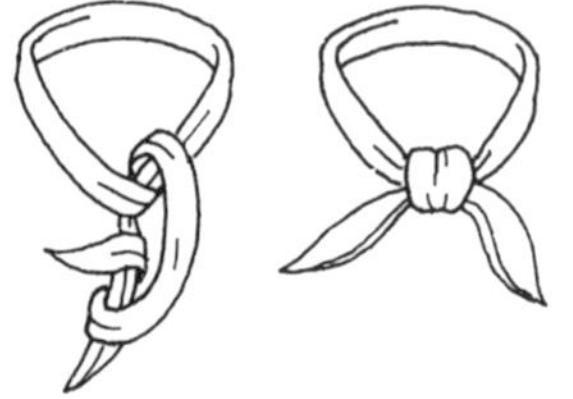

The most essential knot to learn is the square knot, more commonly known as the reef or brownie knot. Work with the longer panel leaving the short panel in place. Place any size scarf around your neck keeping one panel longer about 1-3 inches (2-7 cm). Cross the long panel over the short one and feed up through the neck, creating a single knot. Take the long panel again, over the short panel and feed it through the opening from behind. Pull panels horizontally to desired tightness.

SCARF ACCESSORIES

Using a scarf accessory can make scarf tying more exciting and dramatic. They are easy to use and come in various sizes, finishes, shapes and colours.

ACCENTS

The basic action of the accents are by weaving the fabric in and out through the openings. The decorative face of the accent should not be covered by the sash or scarf.

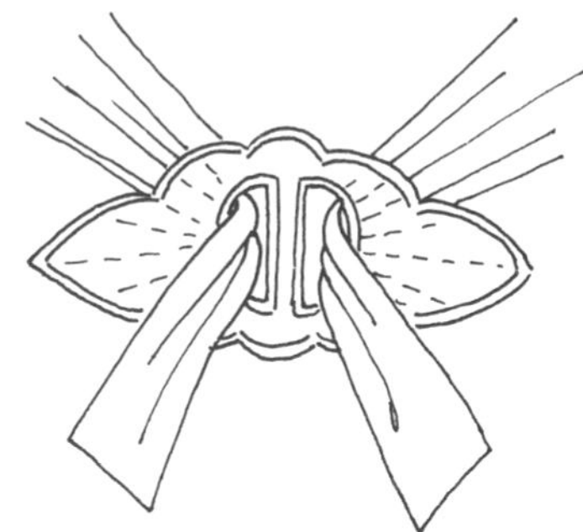

SCARF CLIPS

The versatility of the scarf clip has created a great demand for various types. The sizes and fabrics of your scarves will determine your scarf clip selection. There are 3 basic sizes of loops on the scarf clip. A small loop is good for narrow and light weight scarves. Medium is suitable for most types of scarves and a large loop is ideal for heavier fabrics and larger scarves. The operation of the scarf clip is the same regardless of the size of the loop. Open the scarf clip. Hold it with your thumb on the back of the face, the hinge at the top of your thumb, and your index finger is on the front. Tilt the loop of the clip towards your body when looking in the mirror. Always feed the fabric down through the loop of the scarf clip. When finished with your design, close the scarf clip.

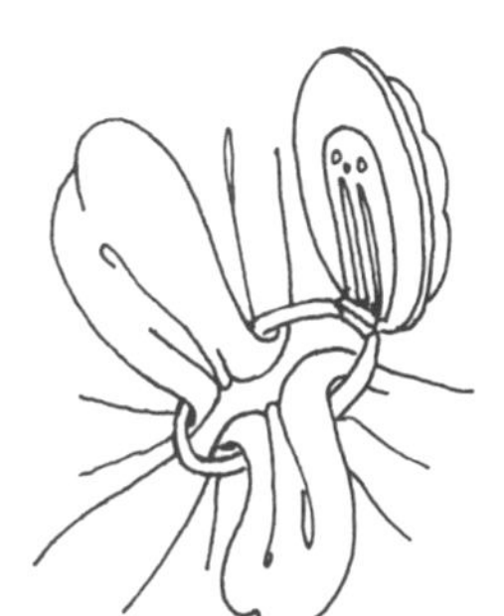

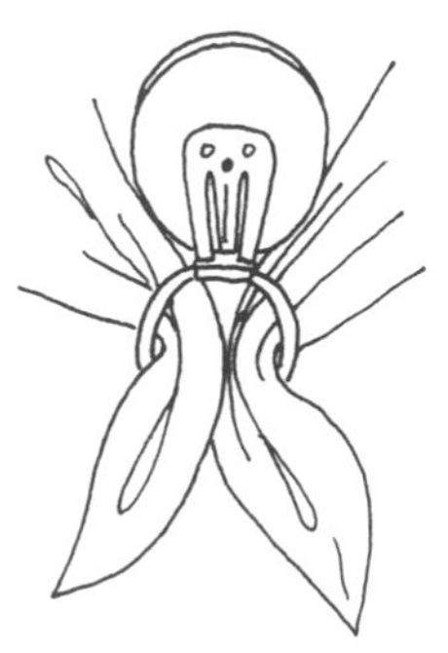

PUFF

Place a bias oblong scarf on a flat surface. With your fingertips, start to pleat from one tip to the other.

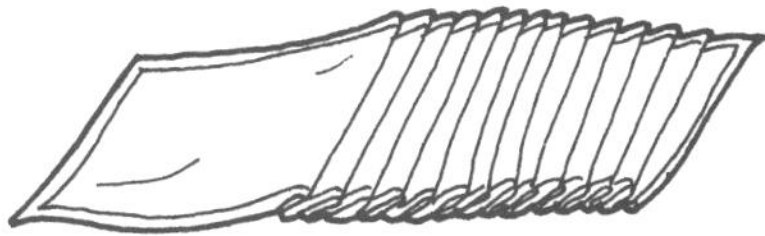

Fold the pleated scarf in half and twist. Stretch an elastic band around the folded scarf to about the centre.

Spread apart the open edges to shape a flower.

Pin to your garment.

BIAS OBLONG

2

POCKET PUFFS

1

Pick up the centre of a small square scarf or pocket puff.

Fold in half.

Place the folded edge into the pocket with puff to the front or place into pocket with the tips featured.

2

Fold a small square scarf or pocket puff in half into a rectangle.

Gather the fabric. Pick up the gathers at the centre and place the folded edge into the pocket.

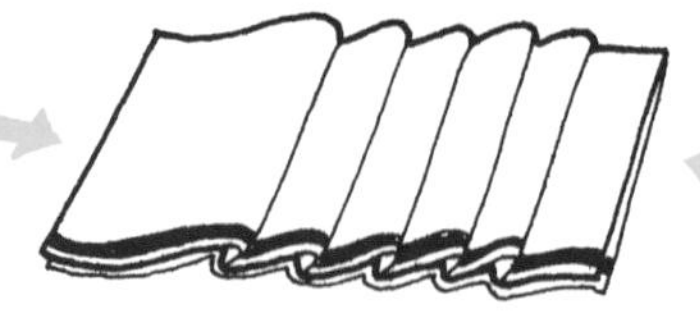

HANDKERCHIEFS

1

Pick up the centre of a small square or handkerchief.

Weave the centre through the openings of your accent from the back to the front.

Pin the accent to your garment and fluff the edges.

2

Pin a safety pin to the underside of your garment to form a bar.

Open a scarf clip. Pick up the centre of the handkerchief and feed down through the loop of the scarf clip. Slide the loop of the scarf clip into the bar.

Take the centre of the handkerchief and pass it over the bar and into the loop of the scarf clip again. Close the scarf clip.

3

Pick up the centre of a handkerchief, gather at the middle and pin it to your garment with a lovely brooch.

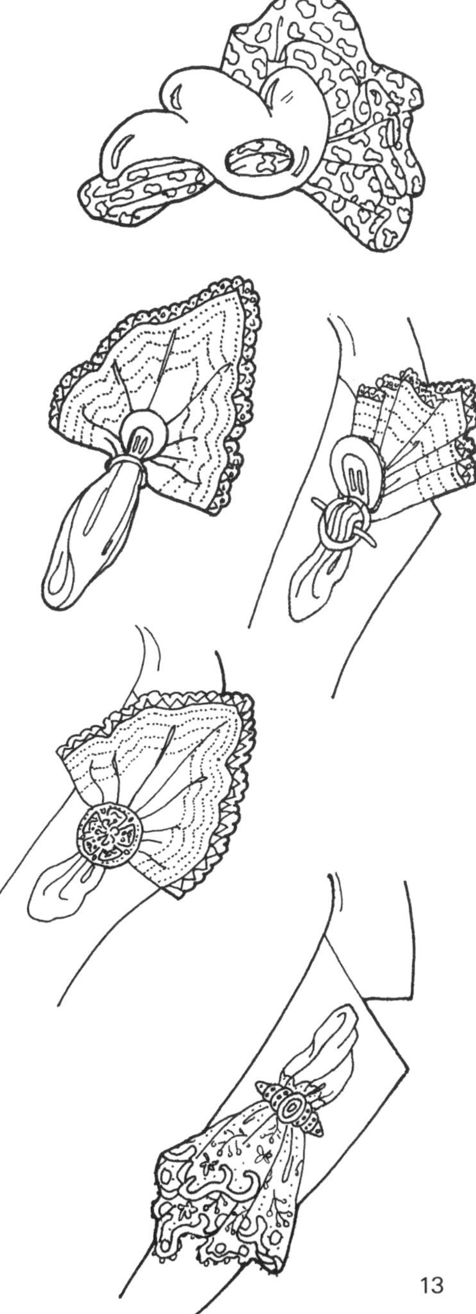

NOTCHED COLLAR

Fold a large square scarf or shawl into a triangle.

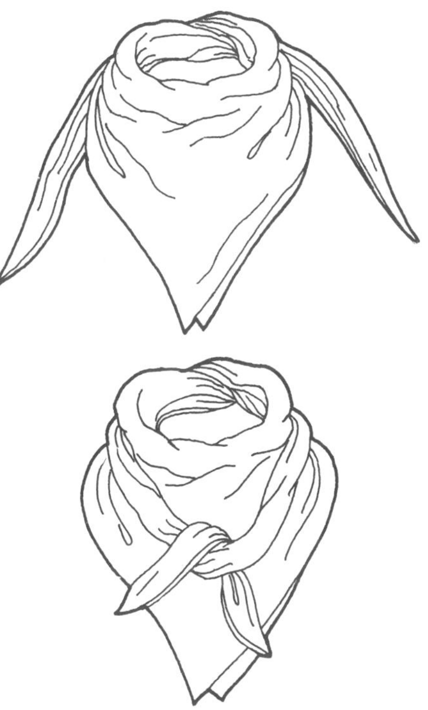

Holding the scarf near the ends, bring your hands closer together draping the scarf into soft folds.

Place the triangle in the front of the neck, criss cross the panels at the back and bring them to the front.

Tie a square knot.

Variation

To form a soft cowl effect, pull the folded edge gently over the knot reducing the size of the triangle.

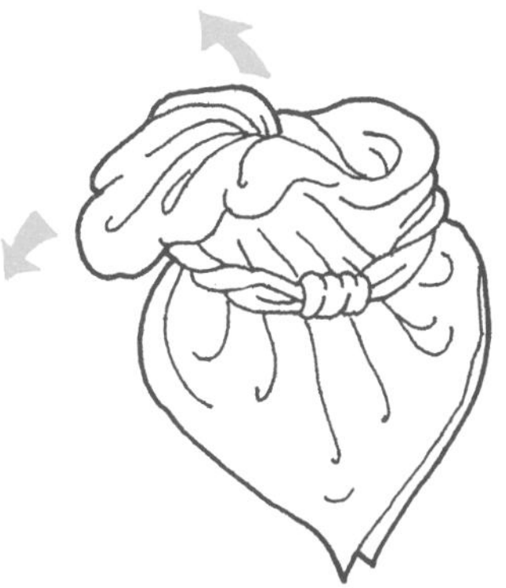

NOTCHED COLLAR

Place a large square scarf on a flat surface. Pick up the centre and tie a rabbit ear knot.

Fold the scarf into a triangle with the knot on the inside.

Place the triangle in the front of the neck, criss cross the panels at the back and bring them to the front.

Tie a square knot with the ends under the triangle. Fluff and arrange for a feminine ascot.

For a smaller square you can simply tie the ends at the back of your neck and tuck the ends in.

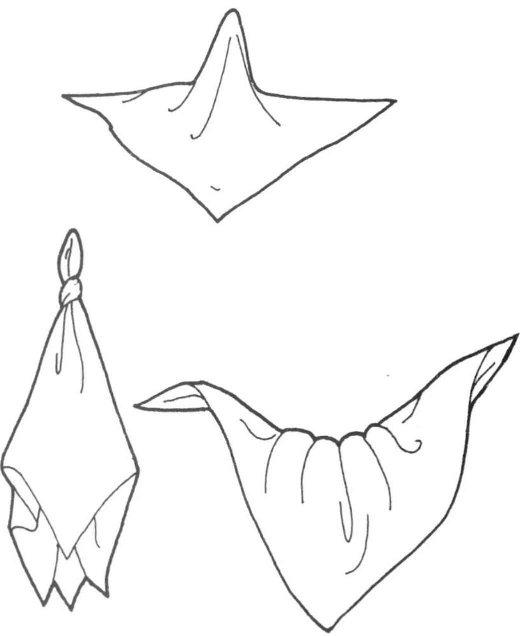

Variation

Follow step 1 as above.

Pick up two corners of a straight edge.

Take the corners to the back of the neck and tie a square knot.

Tuck the ends in.

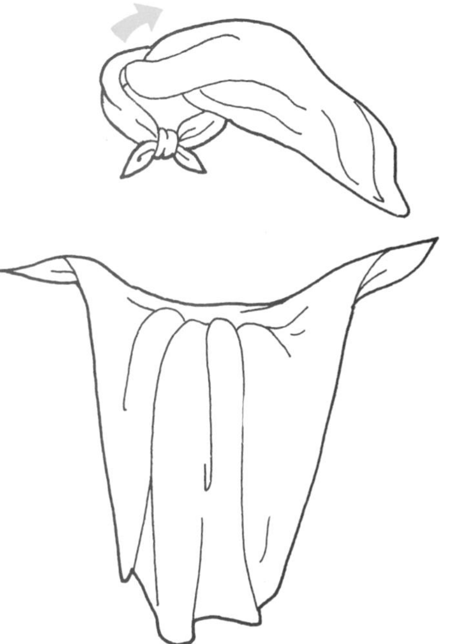

"A soft touch to a tailored look"

FUNNEL NECK

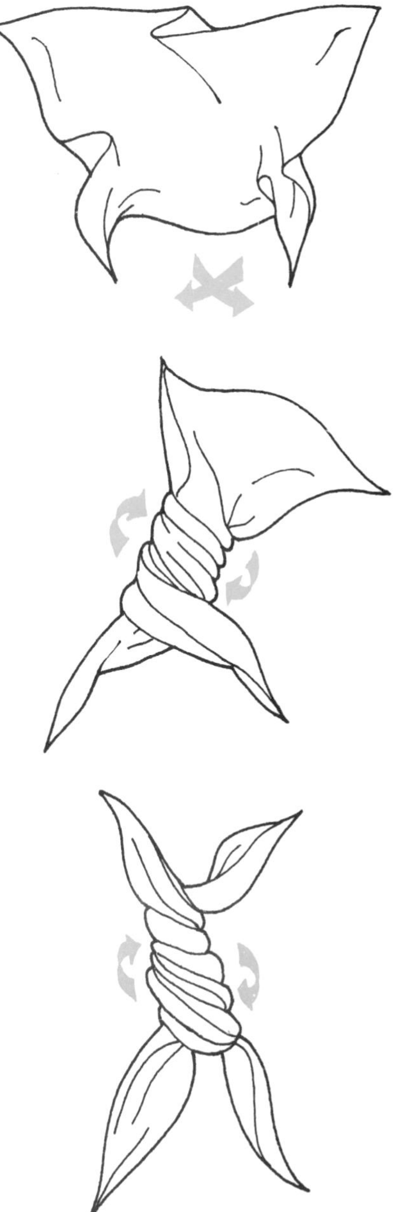

Place a large square shawl on a flat surface. Pick up two corners of a straight edge.

By criss crossing your hands, left over right, twist the shawl with the first twist to the centre. Twist repeatedly until the tension shapes a rope. Anchor the ends to hold the tension.

Pick up the opposite straight edge and criss cross the panels right over the left to the centre, twisting until the tension is uniform.

Pick up the ends of the twisted scarf and place it around your neck. Tie a square knot. Wear off to one side.

Finish the look by adjusting the twists.

"Fit to be tied"

NOTCHED COLLAR (WITH EPAULETTES)

Fold a large square scarf or shawl into a triangle. Feed the scarf through the epaulette from the back to the front with the folded edge towards the neck to almost half way.

If a button is available on the front of the coat, cover it with the scarf and stretch an elastic band around the covered button to secure.

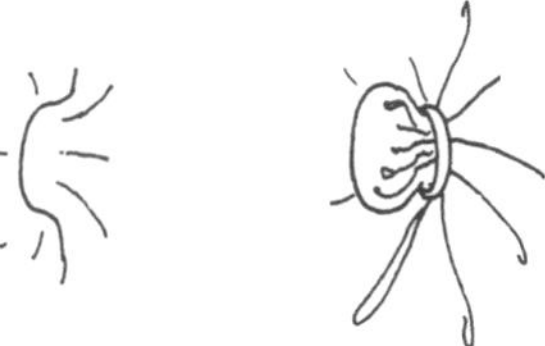

Variation

Feed each panel through the epaulettes from the back to the front. Tuck the ends of the panels inside below the lapels.

8

COSSACK COLLAR

Pin the shawl accent to your garment at the shoulder area.

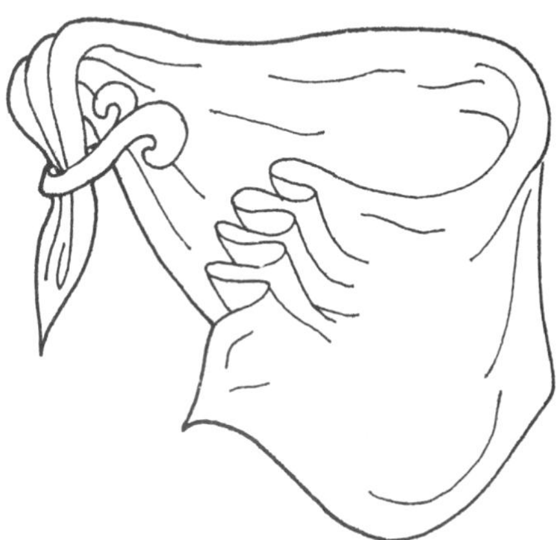

Fold a large square scarf or shawl into a triangle and place the folded edge around your neck. Keep one panel longer.

Feed the short panel through the opening of the accent. Gather the folded edge of the longer panel.

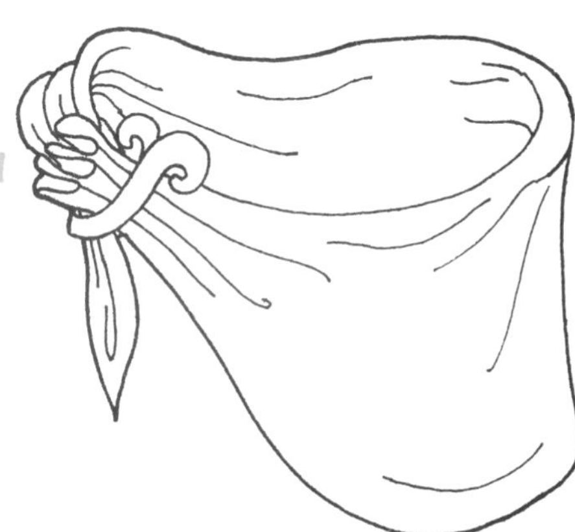

Feed the gathers up through the opening of the accent. Spread the gathers around the accent.

"Beyond tying."

WIDE NOTCHED COLLAR

Fold a large square scarf or shawl into a triangle. Place the centre of the scarf over one shoulder with the ends over the opposite shoulder. Let the end of the front panel fall behind your shoulder.

Feed the back panel through the opening of your accent. Pin the accent to your garment to hold the scarf in place.

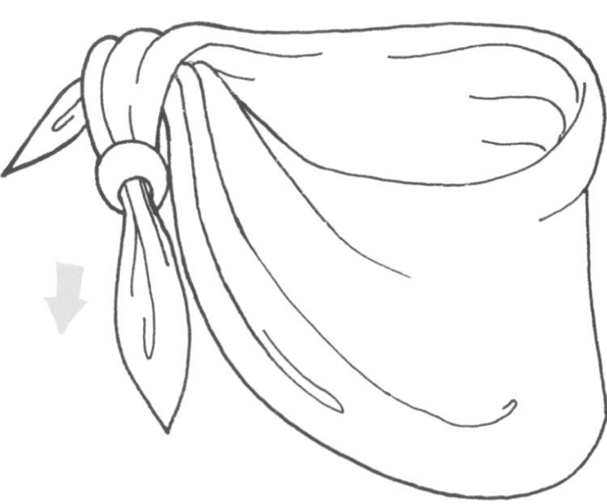

TURTLE NECK

Fold a large square scarf or shawl in half into a rectangle.

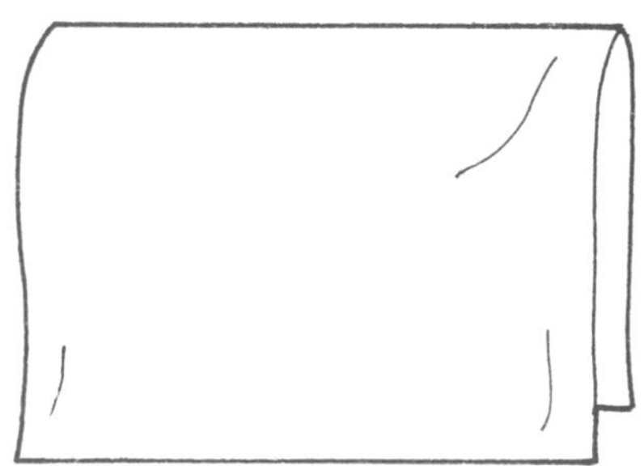

Pick up two opposite diagonal corners to shape two triangles. Place the folded edge next to your neck.

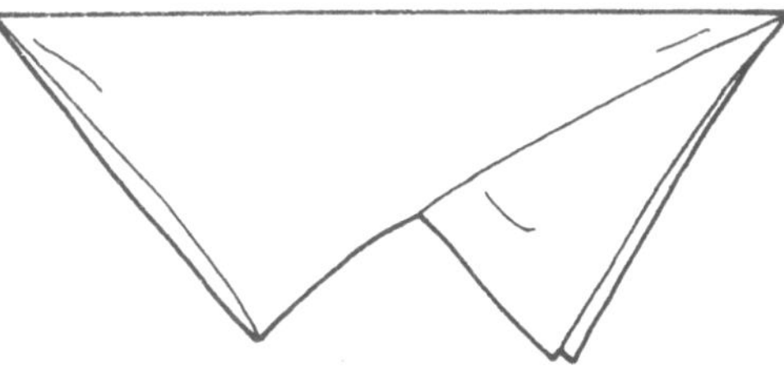

Feed the two ends down through the opening of the accent. Pin the accent to your garment in any desired position.

Adjust and balance the scarf. Spread the panels.

NOTCHED COLLAR

Fold a large square shawl in half into a rectangle.

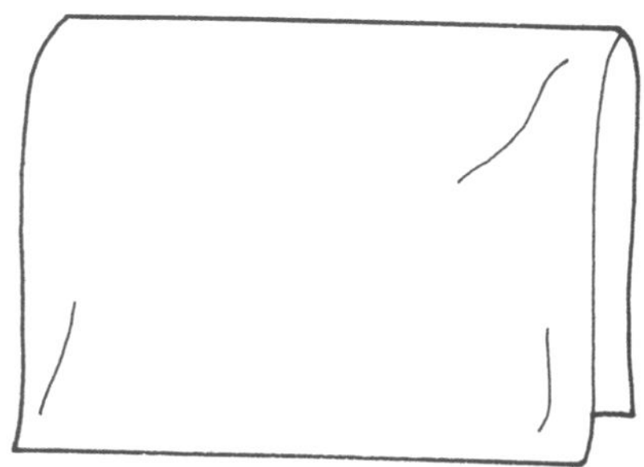

Place the folded edge around your neck keeping the panels even. Pinch the centre of the folded edge.

Feed the pinched edges down through the loop of the scarf clip. Separate the pinched edges to form a bow. Close the clip.

"Update your classics"

12

JEAN JACKET

Fold a large square scarf or shawl into a triangle. Place the folded edge next to your neck, keeping the ends even.

Tie a granny knot by simply taking the ends across the top of the panels and feeding them through the loop from the back to the front.

Pull to tighten.

"A feminine touch to basic workwear"

OPEN JACKET

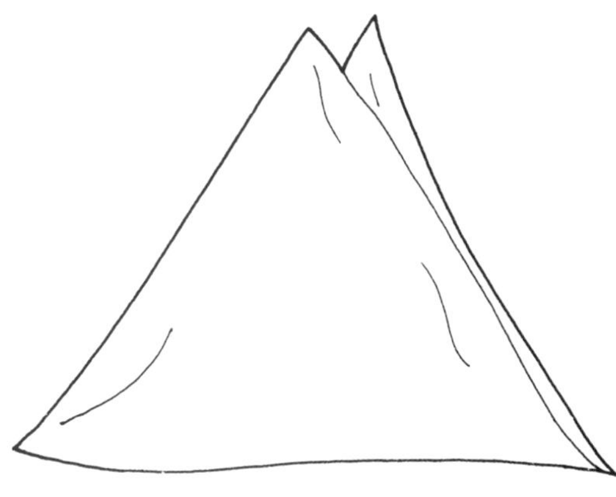

Fold a large square scarf or shawl into a triangle. Take the tips of the open triangle and tie a square knot at the back of your neck.

Fit and gather the folded edge to the waistline. Take the ends to the back and tie a square knot.

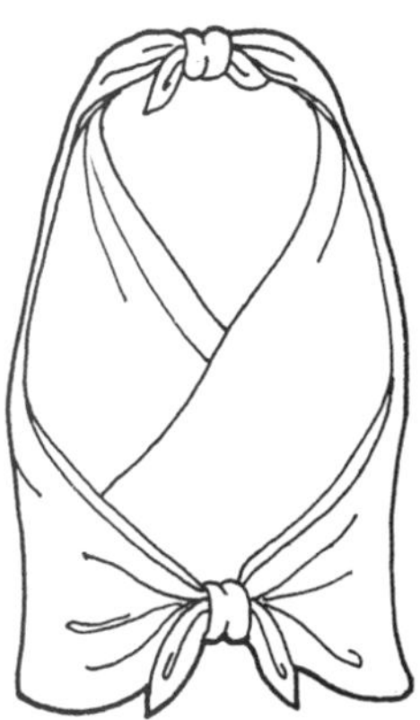

Wear with a jacket as a blouse or as a halter top.

"A great look for the "9 to 5", "After 5" transition"

SQUARE

BLAZER

Fold a large square scarf into a bias. Place the scarf around your neck keeping one panel longer.

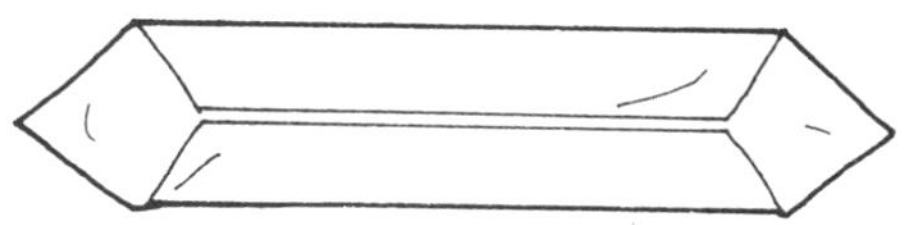

Tie a loose knot with the longer panel by crossing the long panel behind itself and then down into the loop.

Feed the shorter panel down through the loop that you have formed. Adjust and spread smoothly over top of the first panel so that the ends are even.

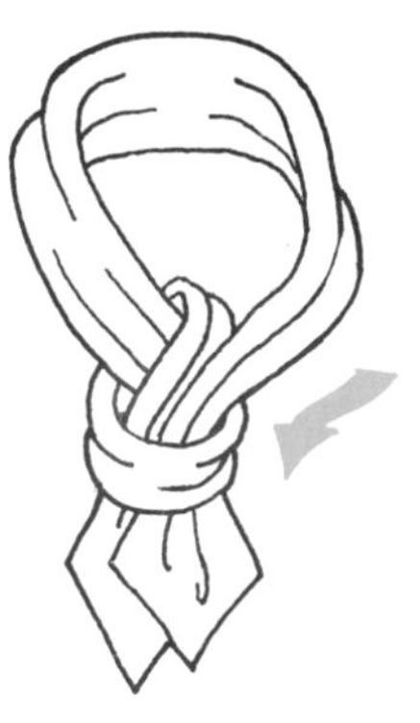

"A crisp, classic, blazer look"

SQUARE

CHANEL NECK

Place an oblong scarf at the front of the neck, criss cross the panels at the back and bring them to the front.

Tie a single knot. Let the panels fall softly.

Variation

Fold a large square scarf in half and continue to fold to a 4 inch (10 cm) width. Place around the neck, tie a single knot and place one panel on top of the other.

"A second life for your Chanel suit"

OBLONG

CHANEL NECK

Place a bias oblong around your neck and tie a square knot, keeping the ends even.

Take the tip of one panel to the knot and hold with one hand.

Feed the folded edge that you have formed up through the neck band half way. This will shape two puffs, one on top of the other.

Repeat with the other panel.

Balance the puffs to an equal size.

"A softer look to Chanel's classic shape"

OBLONG

V-NECK

Fold an oblong scarf into half lengthwise.

Place the scarf around the neckline of your jacket with the open edges next to your neck.

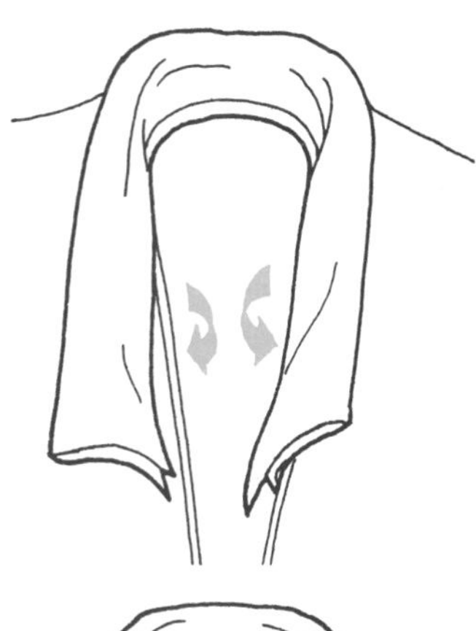

The folded edge is featured to the outside of the jacket and the open edges are tucked underneath to form a collar.

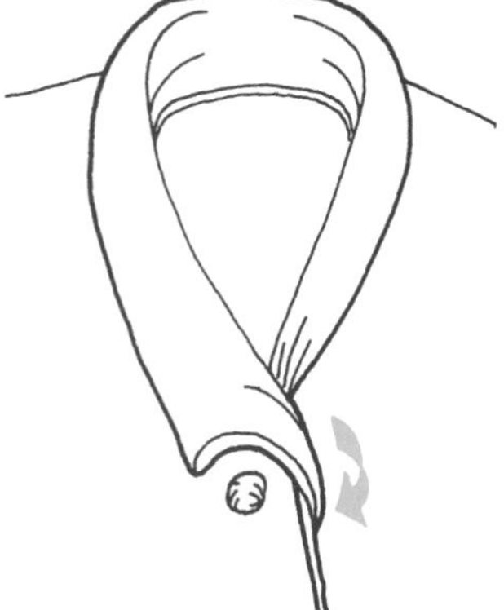

With the panel that follows the line of the button holes, wrap the scarf around the button and then send the covered button through the button hole.

A great way to secure the design.

SHAWL COLLAR

Place a bias scarf on a flat surface.

With your finger tips start to pleat about 10 inches (25 cm) from one end to the same distance from the other end.

Holding the pleats in one hand (keep scarf on the table for support) stretch an elastic band around the pleats to the centre. Fold the pleats one on top of the other.

Pick up the two panels of the scarf and tie a square knot at the back of the neck.

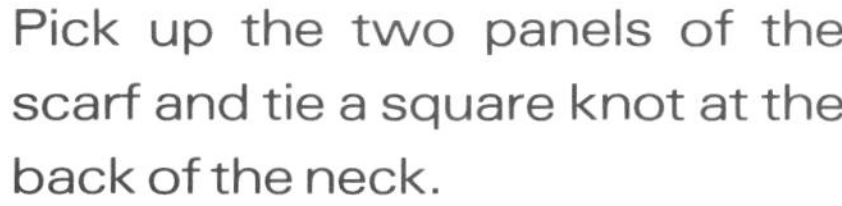

For an added touch of flair, open a scarf clip and clip to the top of the ruffle.

"A great way to soften a severe line in a jacket"

BIAS

19

NOTCHED COLLAR

Fold a large square scarf into a triangle and place the folded edge around your neck. Tie a square knot.

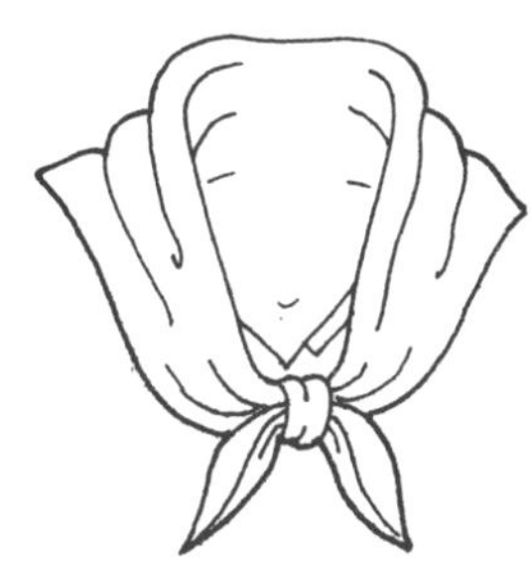

Take the knot to the back of the neck. Pinch the centre of the folded edge.

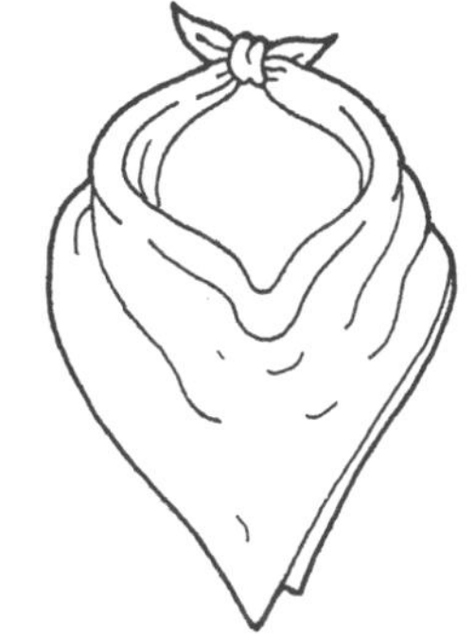

Feed the pinched edge down through the loop of the scarf clip until a puff is formed. Close the scarf clip and spread out the puff.

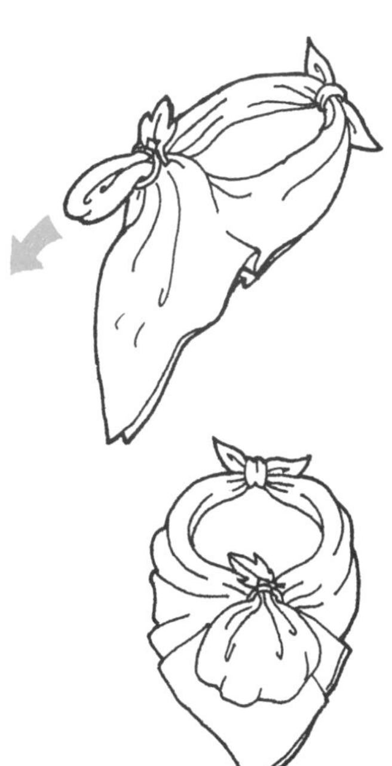

Tuck the triangle inside a suit jacket or blouse, featuring the puff.

NOTCHED COLLAR

Fold a square scarf into a triangle. Place the folded edge next to your neck.

Feed the ends of the scarf down through the loop of the scarf clip. Slide the clip up to your neck.

Spread each panel separately, one on top of the other.

Close the scarf clip.

Tuck the panels into your neckline.

"Definitely worth a second look"

V-NECK

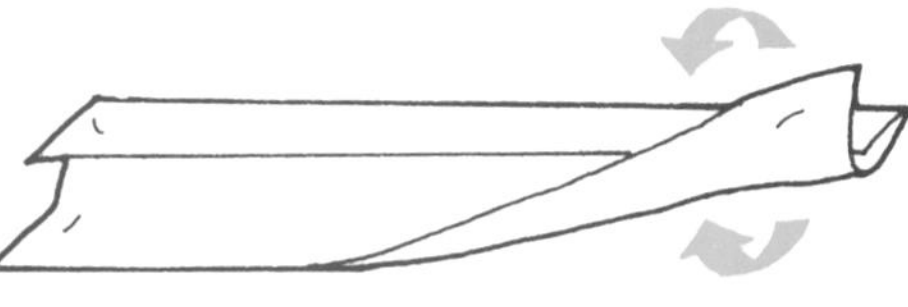

Fold an oblong scarf into thirds lengthwise and place it around your neck. Keep the panels even.

Place one panel over the other.

Place your thumb in behind the centre of both panels and push the scarf down through the loop of the scarf clip about 3 or 4 inches (7 – 10 cm).

With finger tips on the puff, work the scarf through the clip to make the puff a little longer. Close the scarf clip.

Tuck the ends into your jacket.

Variation

Place an oblong scarf around your neck with one panel on top of the other.

Place your thumb in the centre of the back of the two panels and push the scarf down through the loop of the scarf clip. Shape a large puff and pull it to one side of the panels. Close the scarf clip.

Tuck the panels inside your neck-line.

SHAWLS

Fold a large square shawl in half into a rectangle with the right sides together. Tie the open corners together.

Turn the shawl right side out and place your arms through the openings keeping the knots under your arms.

Can be worn as a coverup, shrug, bolero, or evening jacket.

Alternate

Fold the shawl into a triangle. Place the centre of the folded edge on the shoulder and tie a square knot under the opposite arm.

"Totally knaughty"

COWL NECK

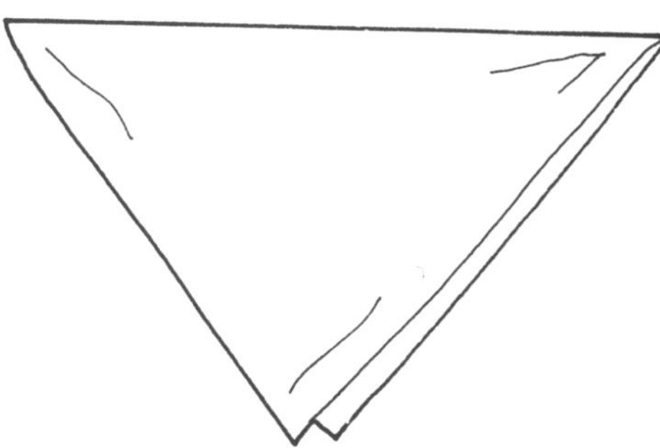

Fold a large square shawl into a triangle and place the folded edge around your shoulders.

Tuck the panels into your waistband or belt.

Variation

Or criss cross the panels in front and take the ends to the back of the waist and tie a square knot.

"Dramatic styling for a plain knit dress"

SQUARE SHAWL

NOTCHED COLLAR

Fold a large square scarf into a triangle. Place the folded edge around your neck keeping the panels even.

Tie a slip knot with one panel.

Pleat the folded edge of the other panel and feed the pleats up through the slip knot.

Pull the end of the slip knot down to tighten.

Fan the pleats.

25

U-NECK

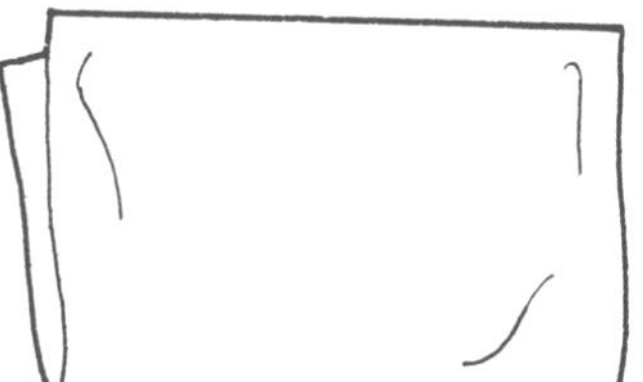

Fold a large square scarf in half into a rectangle.

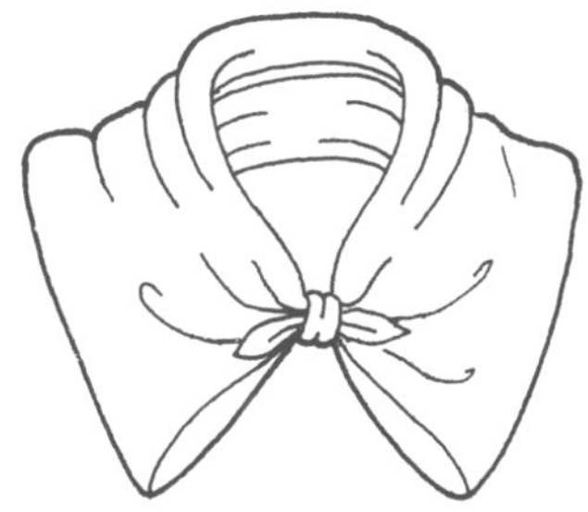

Place the outside edges next to your neck.

Tie a square knot with the open corners.

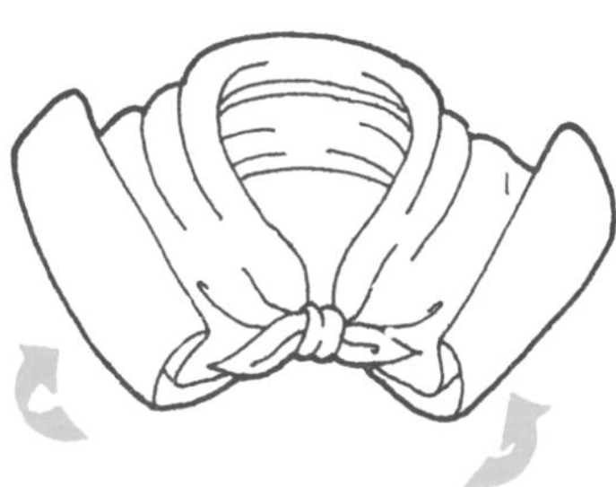

Fold the outside corners towards the neck. Tie a second square knot.

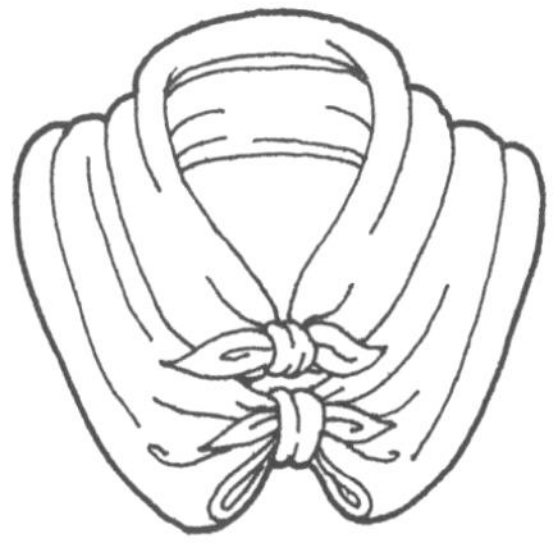

Wear in front as a collar or off to the side for a cowl effect.

SQUARE NECK

Fold a square scarf into a triangle. Place the folded edge next to your neck.

Tuck inside the square neckline as an attractive filler.

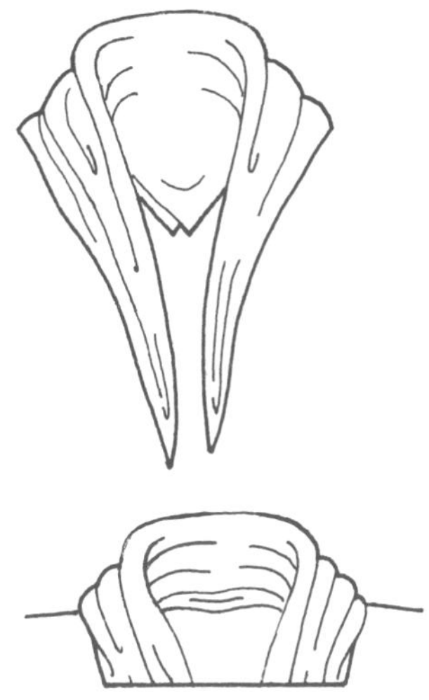

Variation

Fold a square scarf in half into a rectangle. Place the open edges next to your neck.

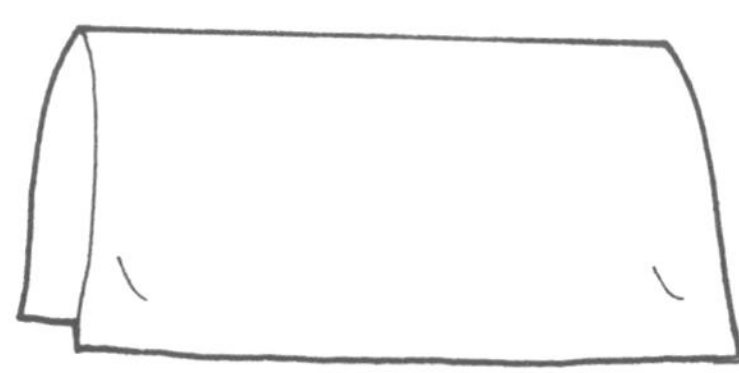

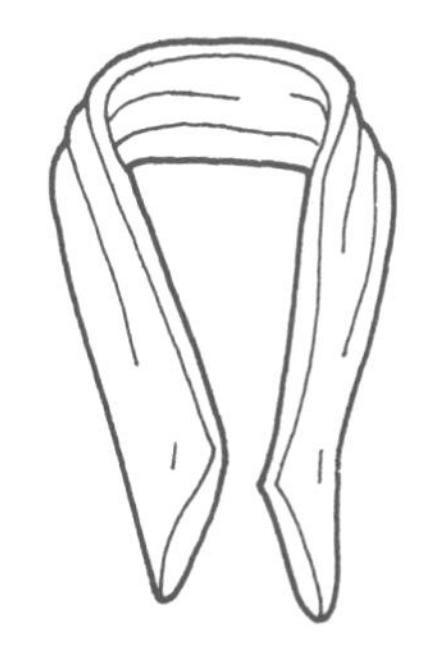

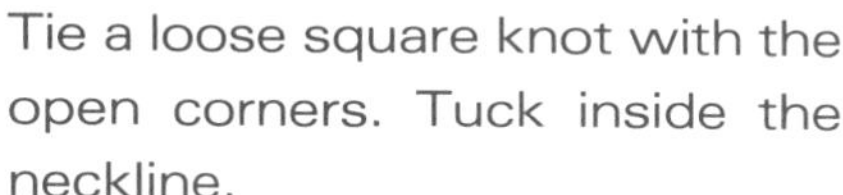

Tie a loose square knot with the open corners. Tuck inside the neckline.

"Especially pretty with a soft chiffon or fine silk scarf"

SQUARE

27

SQUARE NECK

Lay a large square scarf on a flat surface. With your finger tips gather the scarf from end to end. Place the gathered scarf around your neck.

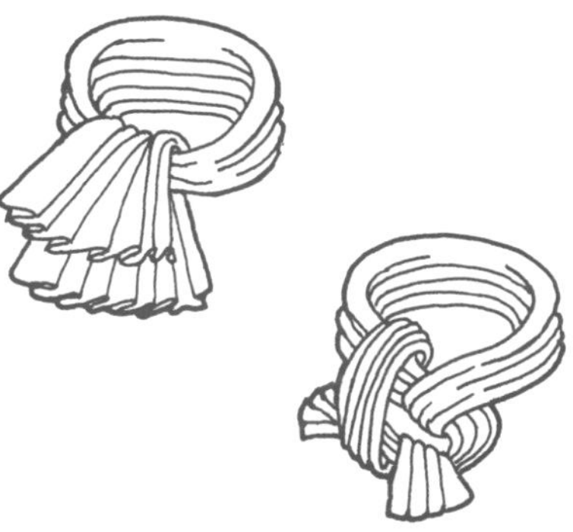

Tie a single knot. Spread and let the gathers fall one on top of the other to create a waterfall.

Variation

For a flower, tie a square knot and bend the sewn edges backwards.

"Properly knaughty"

28

MADARIN COLLAR

Fold a large square scarf into a triangle. Place the folded edge next to your neck and tie a single knot.

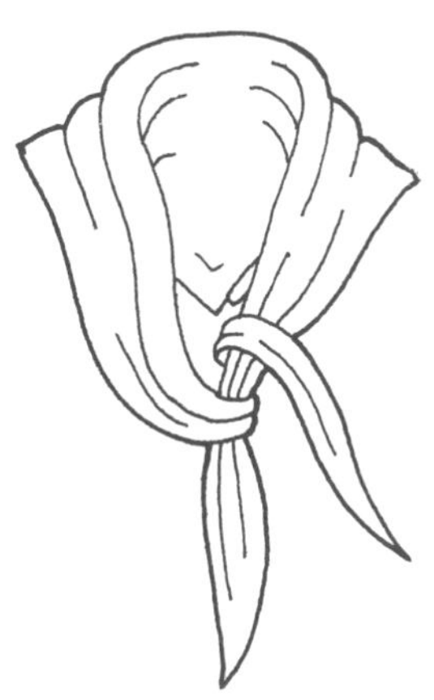

Twist the panels together.

Wrap the twisted panels around itself and tuck the ends into the centre, creating a rosette.

Wear it off to the side or at the centre of a collar.

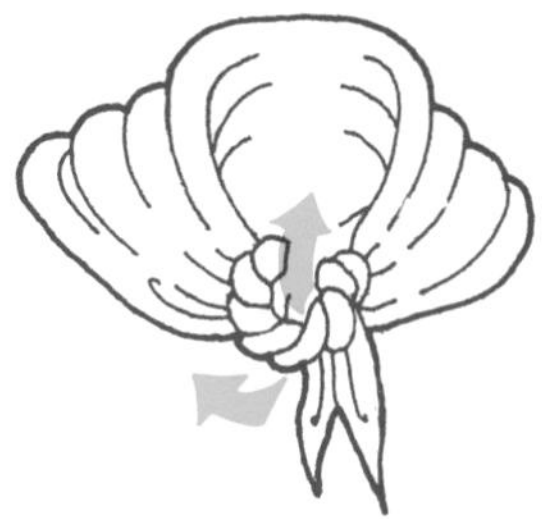

29

JEWEL NECK

Fold an oblong scarf in half into a rectangle.

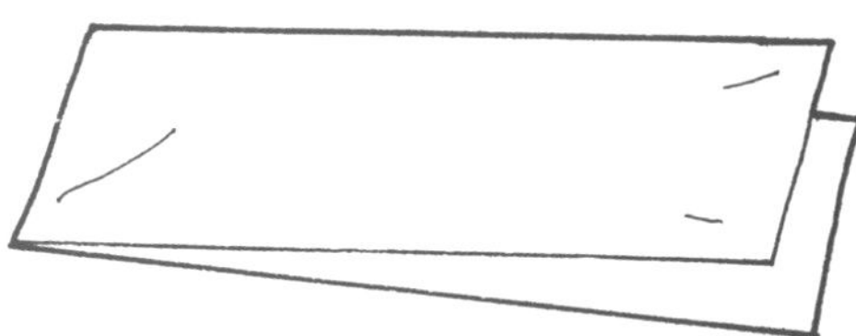

Pick up two opposite diagonal corners to shape two triangles. Place the folded edge around your neck keeping the ends even.

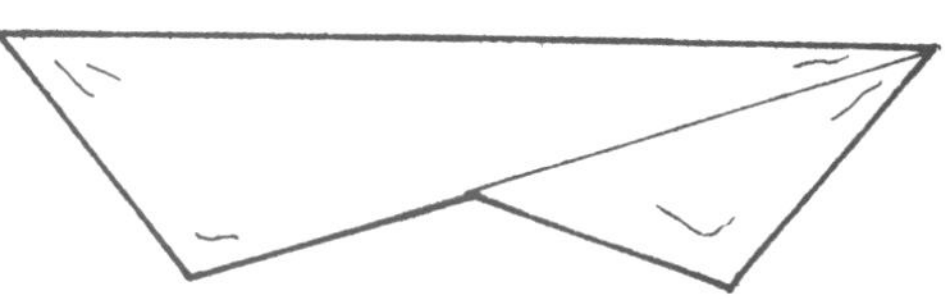

Weave both the ends through the openings of the accent from the back to the front.

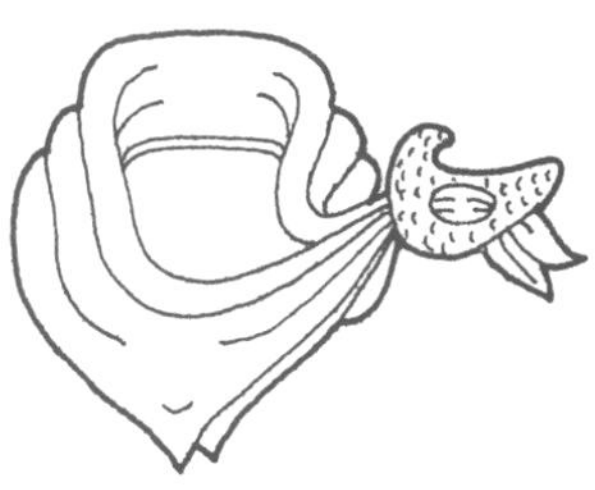

Pin the accent to your garment and arrange your design.

"This one looks great to the side"

30

NOTCHED COLLAR

Fold a large square scarf into a triangle and place the folded edge around your neck. Keep one panel longer.

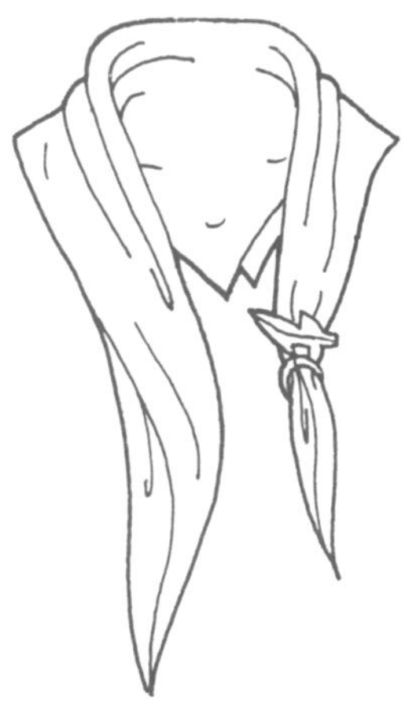

Feed the short panel down through the loop of the scarf clip.

Pinch the centre of the longer panel. Feed the pinched edge down through the loop of the clip to form a half bow. Close the clip.

Spread the ends of the panels.

SCOOP NECK

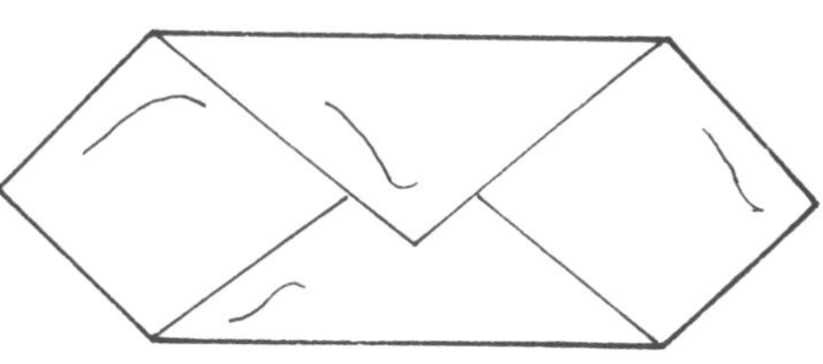

Create a bias shape by using a large square scarf folded three times as shown.

With your fingertips, start to pleat about 10 inches (25 cm) from one end to the same distance from the other end.

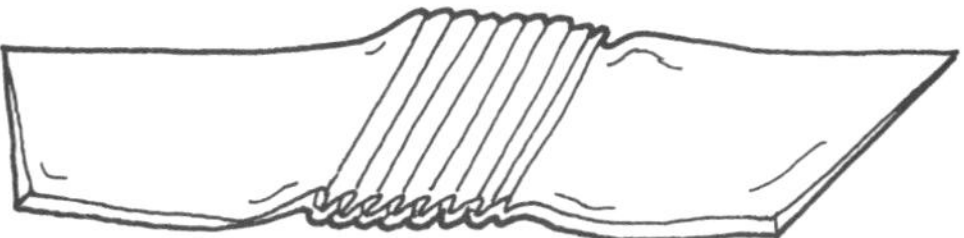

Hold the pleats of the open edge with one hand.

Feed the pleats down through the loop of the scarf clip. Push the clip about one third down the pleats.

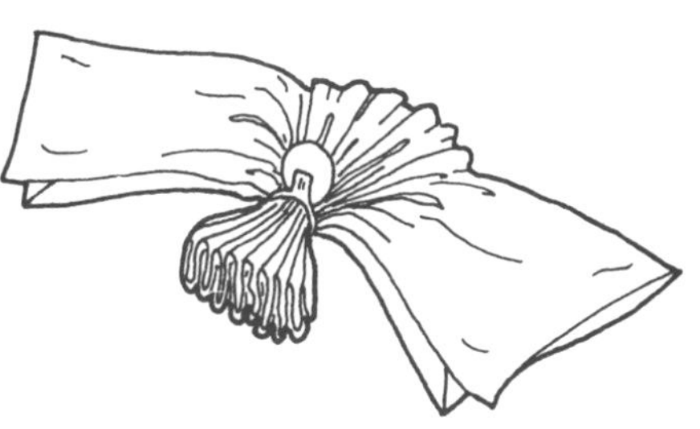

Fold the pleats, the short layer over the longer, with the folded edge of the scarf on the bottom.

Arrange and balance the pleats. Close the scarf clip. Take the ends to the back of the neck and tie a square knot.

"Sensational!"

WINGED COLLAR

Fold a square scarf in half and then in half again.

Place the folded edge next to your neck.

Feed the two centre corners down through the loop of the scarf clip. Work the bottom edges until the outside corners pass through the loop of the clip.

Slide the clip up and close. Arrange the scarf.

COLLAR BAND

Fold a large square scarf into a bias.

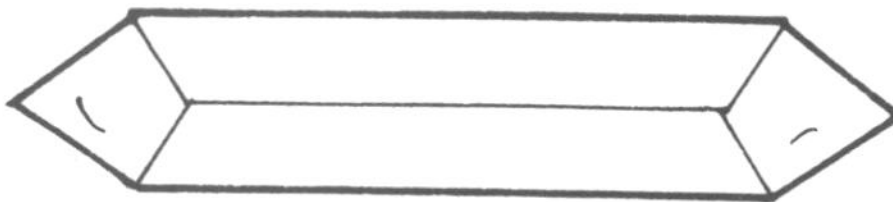

Tie a single knot at the centre of the scarf.

Place the knot in the front of your blouse and pass the panels through the epaulettes. Tie in the back.

Variation

Wrap the ends of your scarf under the epaulette and around the button and let the ends fall freely to the front or back.

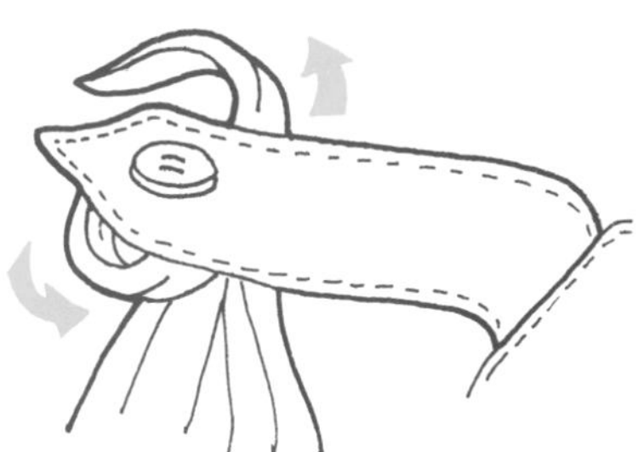

SQUARE

MOCK TURTLE NECK

Twist an oblong scarf and then fold it in half.

Place the twisted scarf around your neck.

Feed the end of one panel through the loop.

Tie a square knot.

Variation

Do not twist the scarf. Simply follow the other steps as above.

35

PETER PAN COLLAR

Place a bias oblong scarf around your neck and tie a square knot.

Feed the tip of one panel through the centre of the square knot. And form a small loop. Repeat with the second panel. Pull loops to tighten.

Variations

Feed the long panel up through the neckline and over the centre of the bow.

To reinforce the single bow, tie a single knot. Or ...

For a flower feed the longer panel over the neckline and tie a second bow. Spread the loops to form petals.

"A tailored look"

BIAS OBLONG

V-NECK

Place an oblong scarf around your neck, keeping the panels even.

Feed both ends through the opening of the accent. Pin the accent to your garment and arrange the scarf loosely.

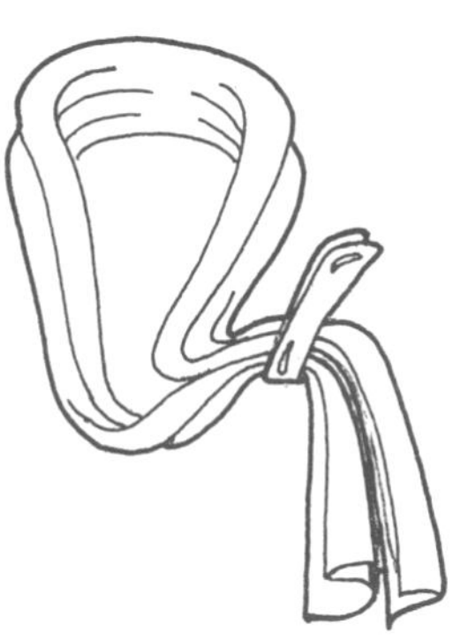

A good design to lengthen a short neck.

JEWEL NECK

Place an oblong scarf around your neck, keeping the panels even.

Feed one panel through each opening of the accent from the back to the front.

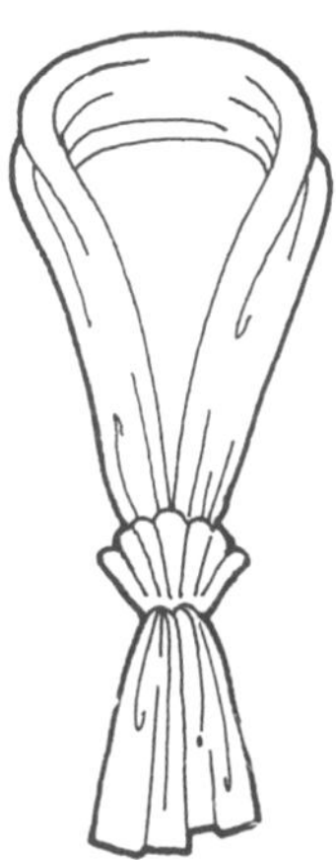

Pin the accent at the centre of your neckline. Adjust the length of the panels to create a soft collar.

"A pretty addition to a basic "Office" Look"

OBLONG

38

CHELSEA NECK

Fold a square scarf into a bias.

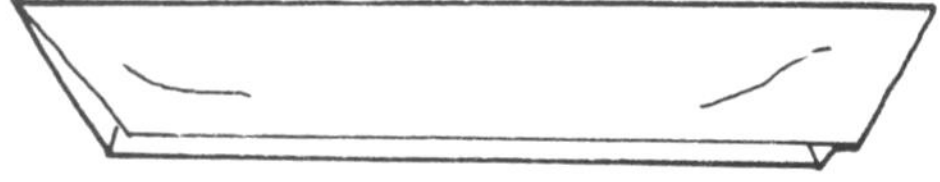

Weave one end through the openings of the accent from the back to the front.

Slide the accent to the centre of the scarf.

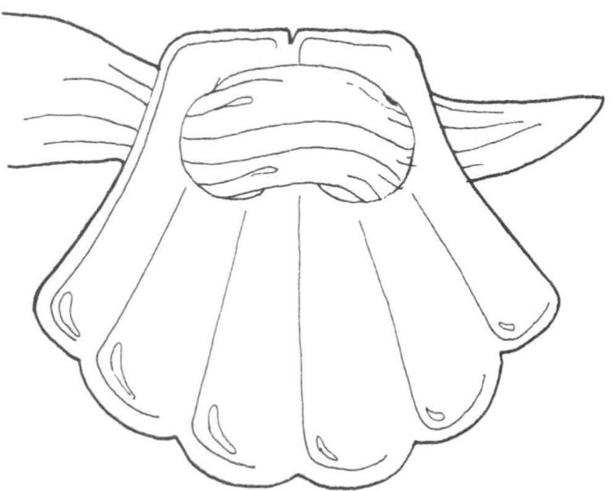

Place the accent at the front of your neckline. Take the panels to the back of the neck and tie a square knot.

Lovely with a collar.

Variation

Place the scarf around your neck.

Feed one panel through each opening of the accent from the back to the front.

Pin the accent to your garment off to the side.

39

PETER PAN COLLAR

Place a narrow tie or bias scarf around the neck keeping the ends even.

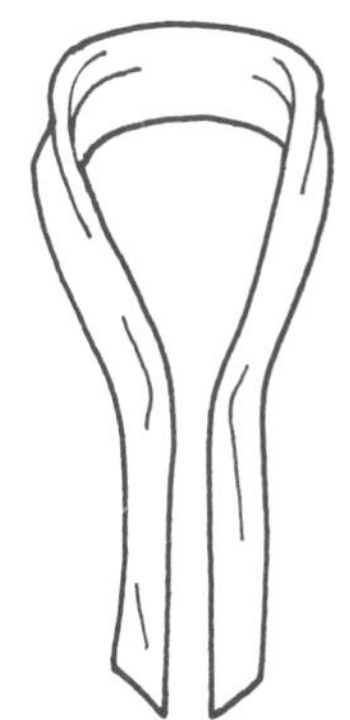

Pinch the inside edges about half way down from the neck.

Feed the pinched edges down through the loop of the scarf clip.

Separate and spread each fold to form a bow.

Close the scarf clip.

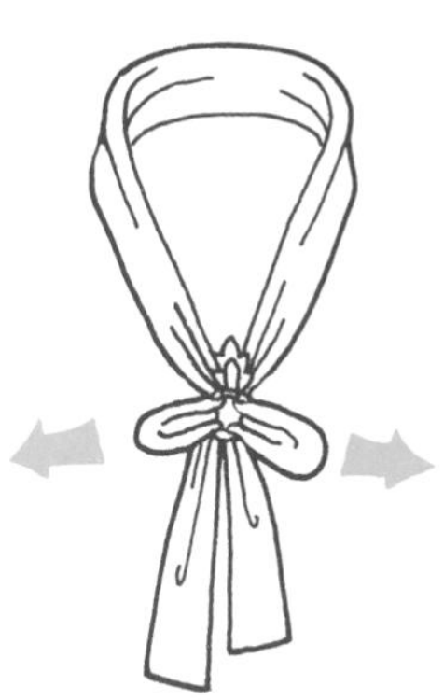

"A perfect bow every time"

TIE OR BIAS SCARF

40

NOTCHED COLLAR

Fold a large oblong in half lengthwise. Place the folded edge around the neck keeping the ends even.

Pinch the centre of the folded edge halfway down from the neck.

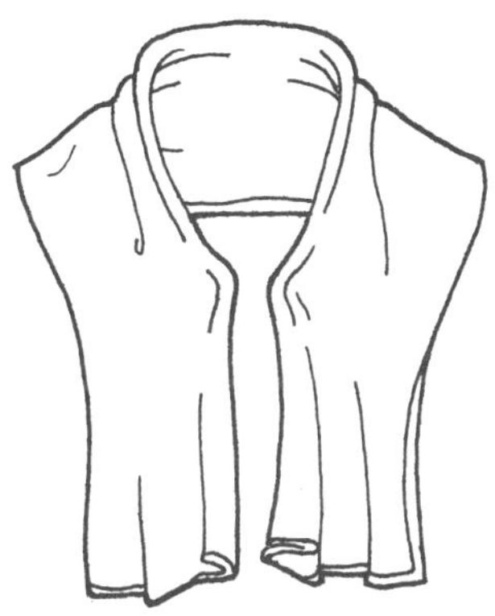

Feed the pinched edges down through the loop of the scarf clip. Separate the pinched edges and work the top of the loops until you have formed two large puffs. Close the scarf clip.

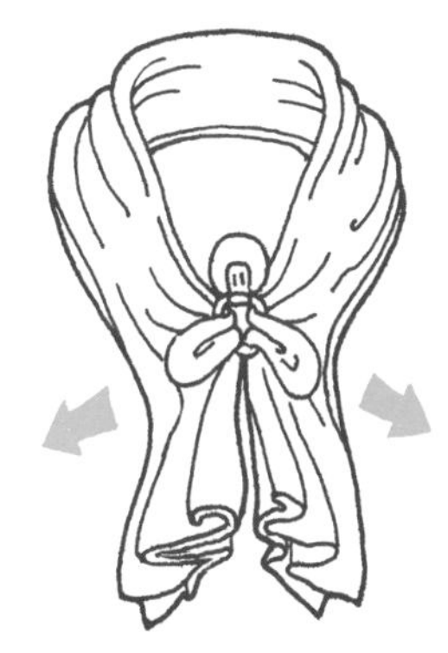

"Soft and feminine, especially with a chiffon scarf"

OVERSIZED OBLONG

V-NECK

Fold an oblong scarf into thirds lengthwise. Place the scarf at the front of the neck, criss cross the panels at the back and bring them to the front keeping one panel longer.

Tie a single knot. Arrange panels one on top of the other.

Tuck the panels inside a blouse or sweater.

Add an attractive necklace to compliment your look.

TURTLE NECK

Place a bias oblong scarf at the front of the neck, criss cross the panels at the back and bring them to the front.

Loosen the loop away from the neck. Tie a single knot with the ends.

Place the single knot above at the centre of the loop.

Tie another single knot to form a square knot holding the loop in place. Holds beautifully.

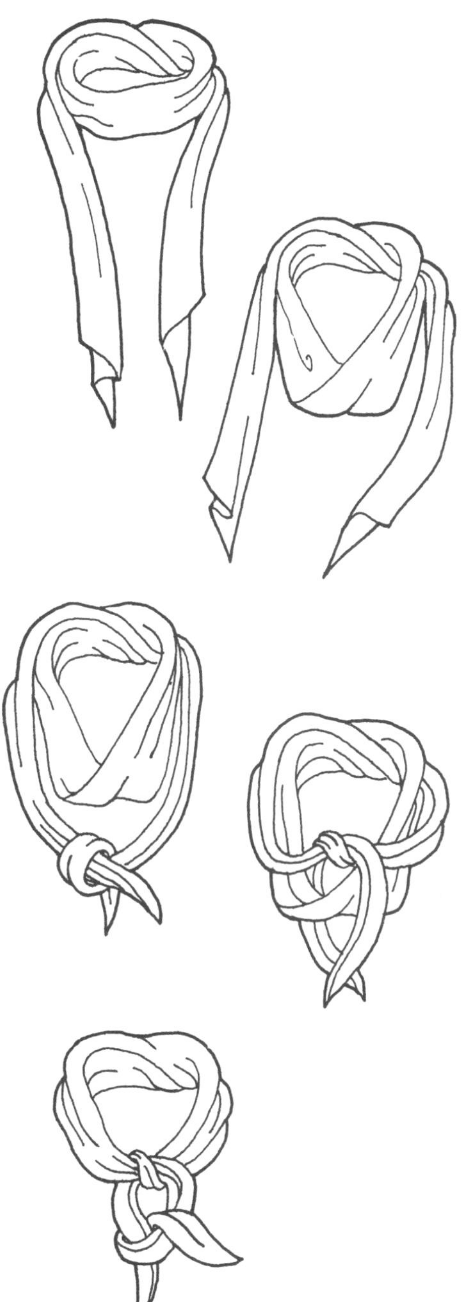

"Looks difficult – but worth it"

BIAS OBLONG

FUNNEL NECK

Fold a large square scarf into a bias.

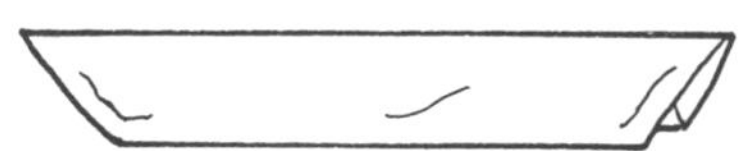

Twist the scarf and wrap around the neck.

Tie a square knot.

Variation

When using a longer scarf wrap it around the neck twice.

"A sporty look with a bulky sweater"

BANDANA

V-NECK

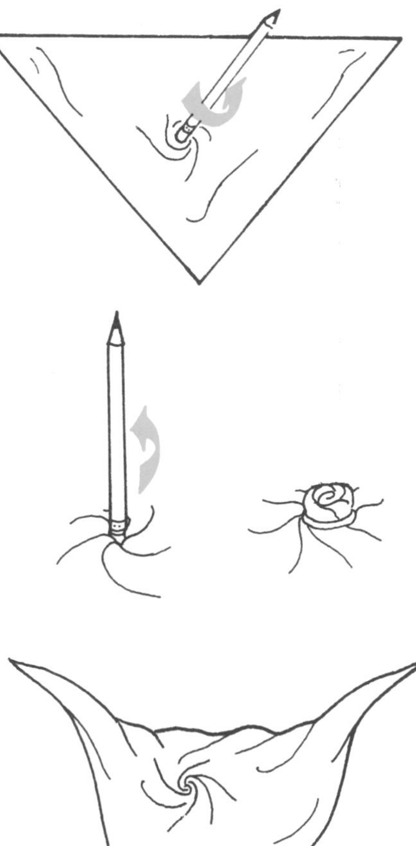

Fold a large square scarf into a triangle. Lay on a flat surface.

Place and hold the rubber tip end of a pencil one third of the way from the folded edge of the scarf. Twist the pencil in circles to form a rosette.

While removing the pencil, hold the rosette with one hand and secure with a small elastic band.

Place the scarf around your neck with the rosette in the front. Criss cross the panels at the back and bring them to the front. Tie a knot under the triangle. Let the rosette drape softly over the knot.

If using a small square scarf, tie the knot at the back of the neck and tuck the ends in.

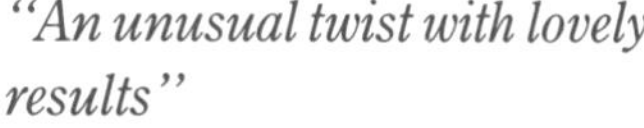

"An unusual twist with lovely results"

SQUARE

ROLL COLLAR

Place an oblong scarf around your neck keeping one panel longer. Working with the longer panel, tie a single knot.

Wrap the longer panel around the neck band again and then down through the loop that you have formed.

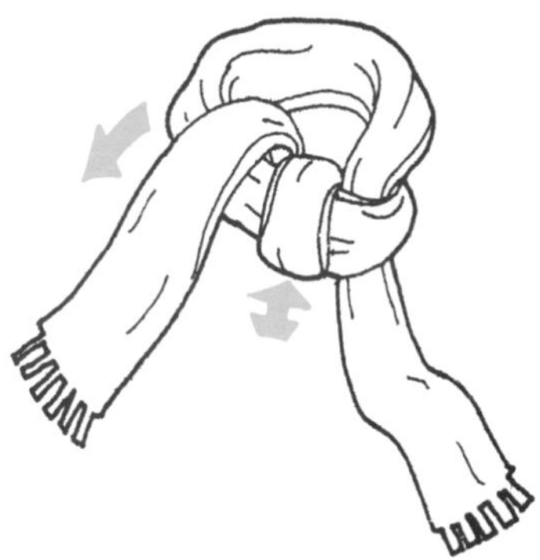

Smooth and arrange the panels.

Great with a sweater.

"Tying with flair."

FUNNEL NECK

Place an oversize textured oblong around the neck keeping one end longer.

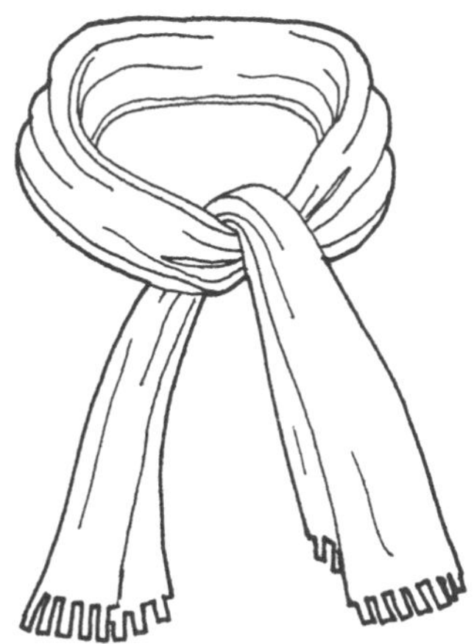

Tie a single knot.

Take the longer panel and wind it around the neck area of the scarf two or three times.

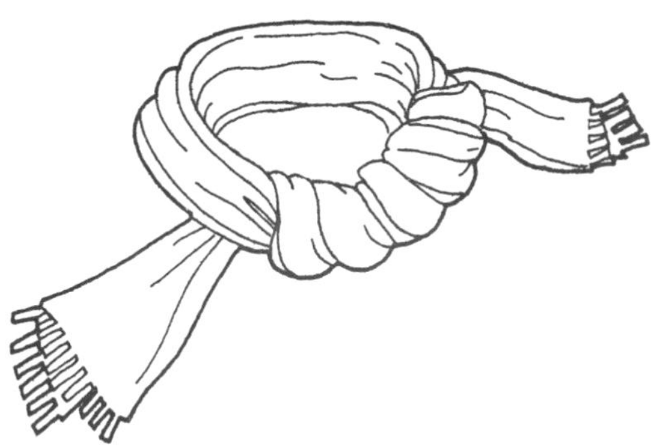

Repeat with other panel winding only once.

"A soft, wool muffler wound loosely looks cozy."

OBLONG

BOAT NECK

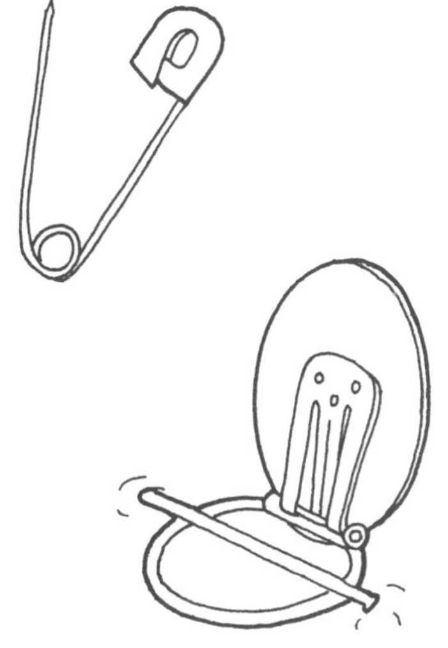

Place a safety pin on the underside of your garment, close to the neckline on the shoulder.

Place an oblong scarf around your neck keeping one panel shorter. Take the short panel down through the loop of the scarf clip. Feed the loop of the scarf clip through the safety pin.

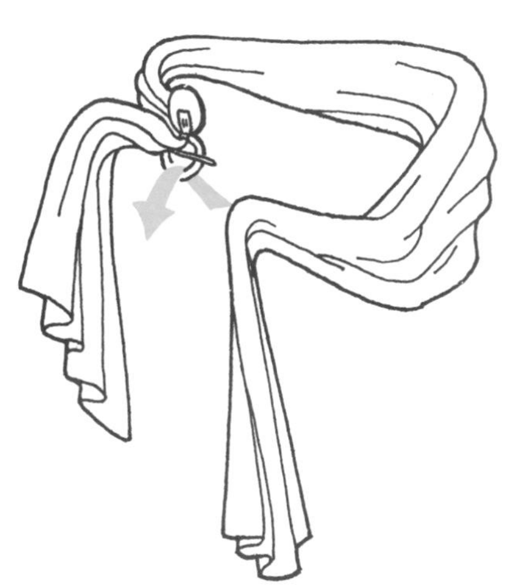

Pinch the centre of the longer panel and feed it through the loop of the scarf clip below the pin.

Close the scarf clip.

Spread the puff you have formed and balance the ends.

This technique secures the design.

"A graceful neckline for those with a longer neck"

OBLONG

48

CONVERTIBLE COLLAR

Fold a bandana into a triangle. Roll the folded edge once, about 2 inches (5 cm) to create a collar.

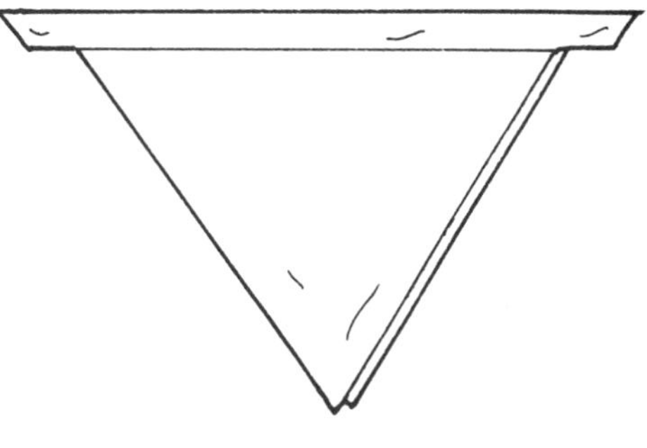

Place the scarf around your neck with the triangle in front.

Tie a square knot at the back of your neck.

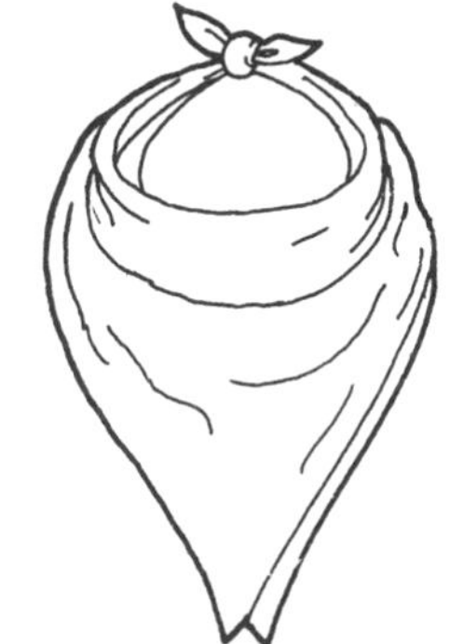

Tuck inside your shirt or blouse.

Variation

Use a large square scarf outside a jacket.

BANDANA

49

CREW NECK SWEATSHIRT

Fold a large square scarf into a bias.

Place it around your neck. Tie a loose square knot.

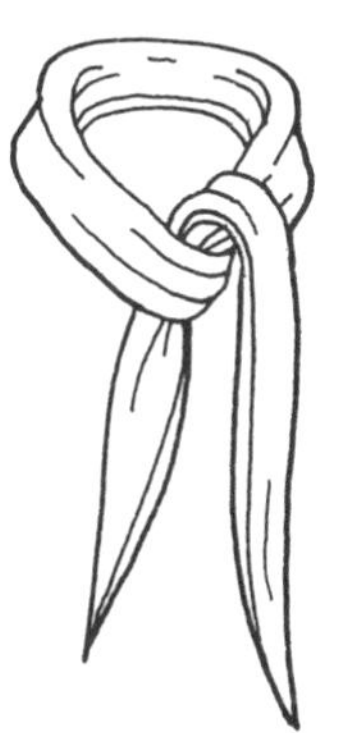

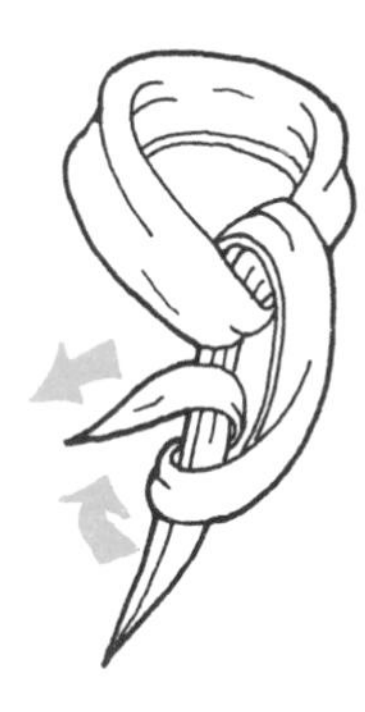

Bring the panels to the back of the neck and tie a second square knot. Tuck in the ends.

Variation

For a more casual look leave the ends hanging in the front.

"A stylish look for 'Sweats'"

50

CONVERTIBLE COLLAR

Fold a large square scarf into a bias.

Make a loose knot in the centre.

Tie two more knots on either side of the centre knot. Keep the knots evenly spaced, and consistent in size.

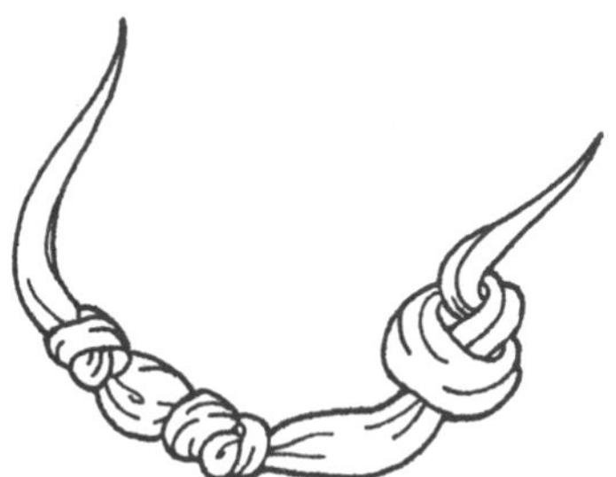

Take the ends to the back of the neck and tie a square knot.

"Lots of knots"

SQUARE

CONVERTIBLE COLLAR

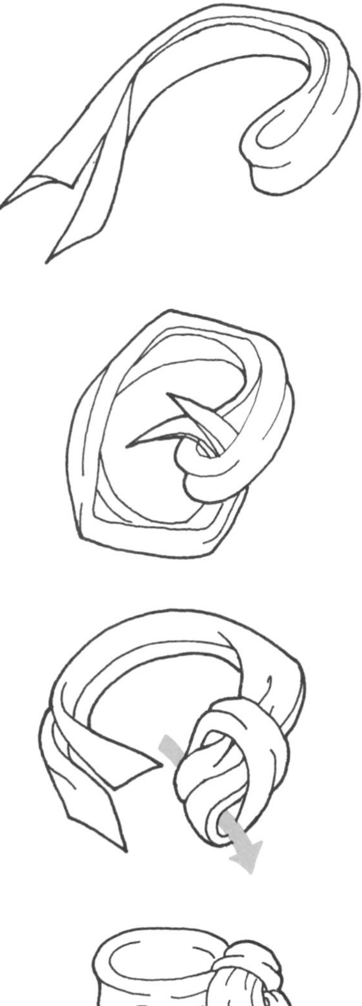

Fold a bias oblong in half. Hold the scarf at the fold and feed the ends through forming a circle. Hold the circle loosely with one hand, continue to pull the ends through forming a loop.

Keep your fingers in the loop and place the scarf around your neck. Feed the ends of the panels through the loop where your fingers are. Adjust the panels.

Variation

Tuck the ends of the panels back through the neckline.

SCOOP NECK

Place an oblong scarf around your neck keeping the ends even.

Twist the panels around each other twice.

Take the ends of the panels to the back of the neck and tie a square knot.

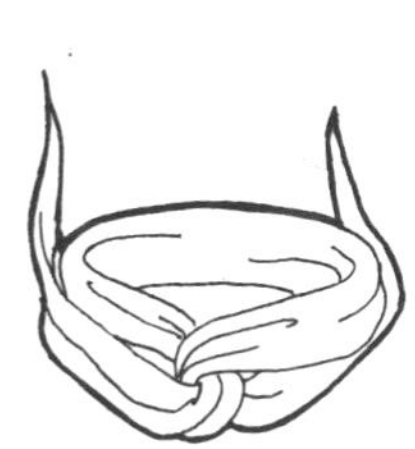

Alternate

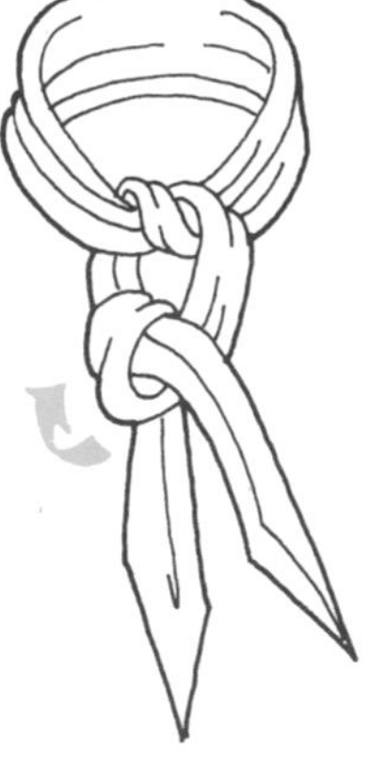

Tie a single knot repeatedly to the ends of the panels.

Can also be done on a large square scarf folded into a bias.

Secure with an attractive brooch.

Pretty on a scoop neck.

GOLF SHIRT

Tie a loose single knot about 6 inches (15 cm) from one end.

Work with the long panel by forming a loop near the knot and feed it through the knot.

Continue making loops to form a chain, leaving about 6 inches (15 cm) for finishing.

Take this end and send it through the last loop and tighten to secure the chain.

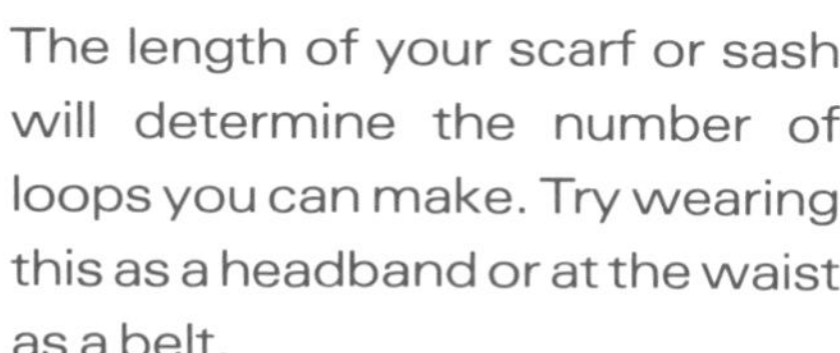

The length of your scarf or sash will determine the number of loops you can make. Try wearing this as a headband or at the waist as a belt.

54

CREW NECK SWEATSHIRT

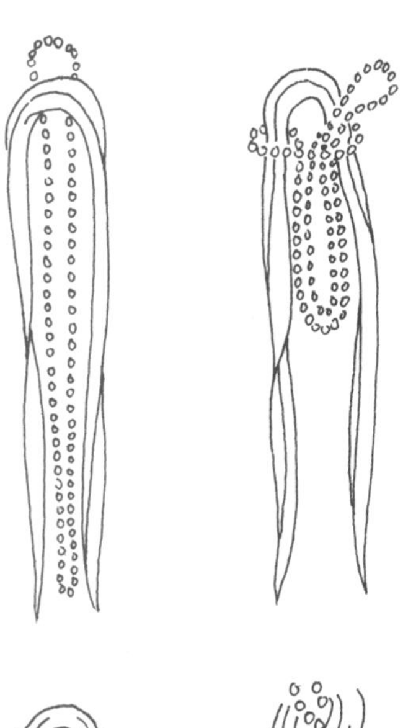

Fold a long narrow scarf in half.

Link a long strand of beads with the loop of the scarf.

Braid the two panels and the string of beads.

Place around the neck and feed one panel of the scarf through the end loop of the beads.

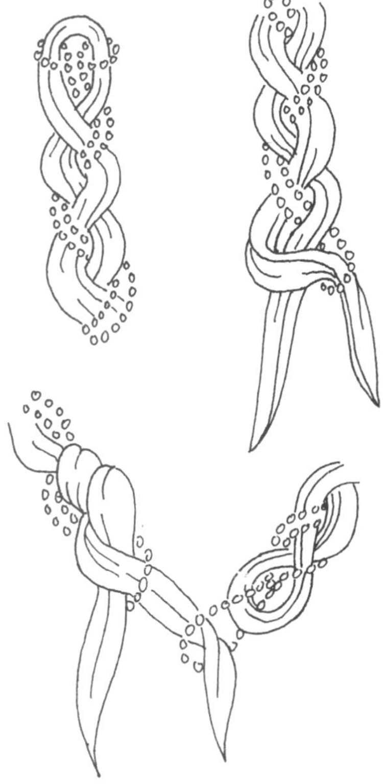

Tie a square knot.

"Tie it together."

LONG BIAS, OBLONG OR SASH

55

BOAT NECK

Fold a small square scarf or bandana into a triangle.

Place around your neck keeping the panels even.

Feed both the ends down through the loop of the scarf clip. Slide the clip up.

Twist each panel so the folded edges are on the outside toward your arms.

Take one tip of the scarf and feed it down the loop of the scarf clip again, just an inch or two (2 to 5 cm).

Repeat with the other tip. Close the scarf clip. Spread both sides of the bow.

"Smooth sailing"

T SHIRT

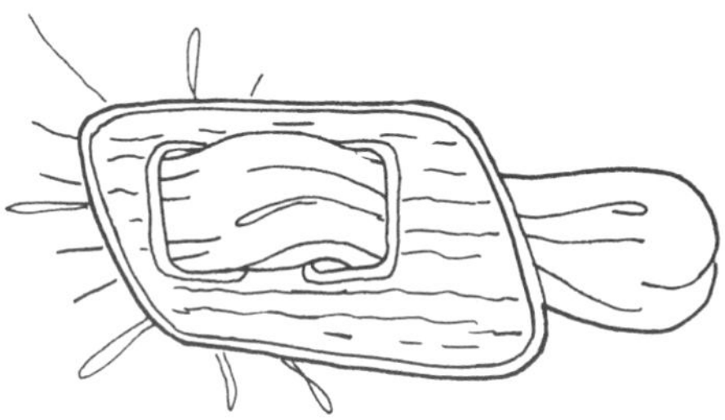

Pinch the fabric of your T shirt and weave through the accent from the back to the front. Spread the end.

Variation

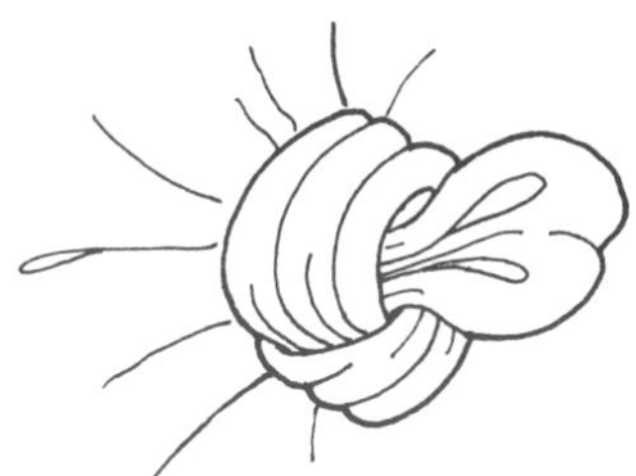

Pick up the hem of your T shirt. Gather and stretch the fabric around your fingers and form a knot.

Variation

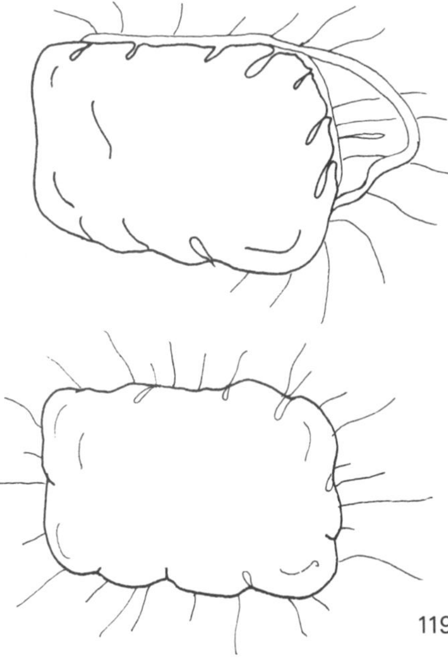

Place the accent on the underside of your T shirt. Hold the T shirt around the accent together from the outside.

Stretch an elastic band around the covered accent.

NOTCHED COLLAR

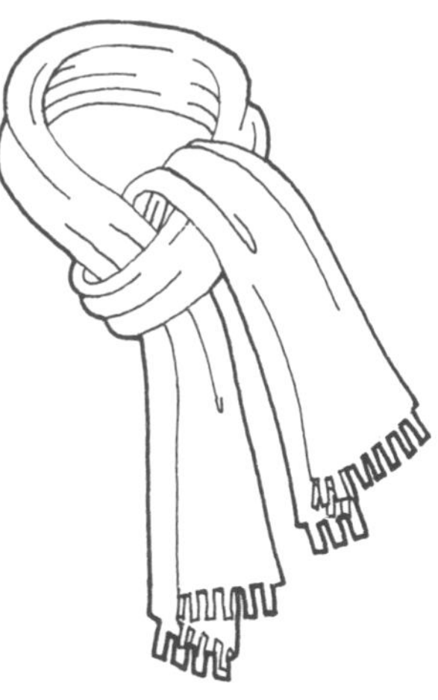

Place an oblong scarf around your neck.

Tie a single knot.

Spread the top panel over the bottom one.

Wear under or over top of jacket or coat.

FUR COLLAR

Fold a textured oblong scarf in half and place it around your neck.

Feed one panel behind and then through the loop.

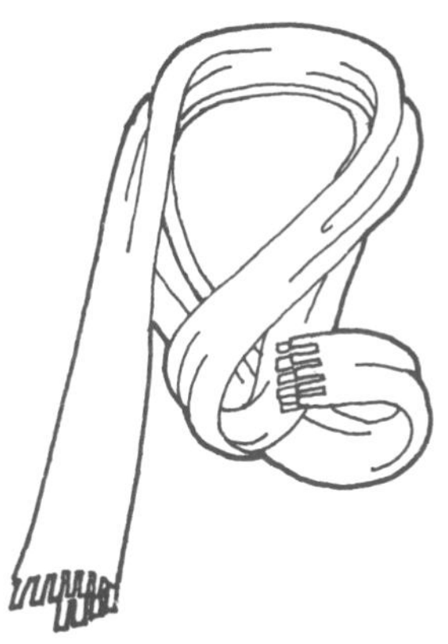

Feed the other panel through the loop from the top.

Finish the design by adjusting the panels.

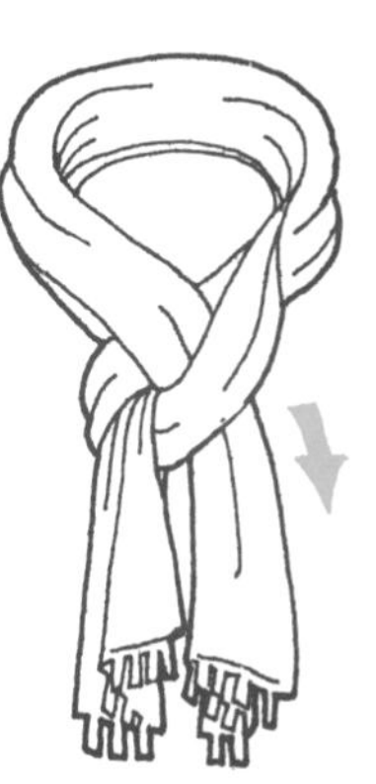

Can be worn inside or outside a jacket.

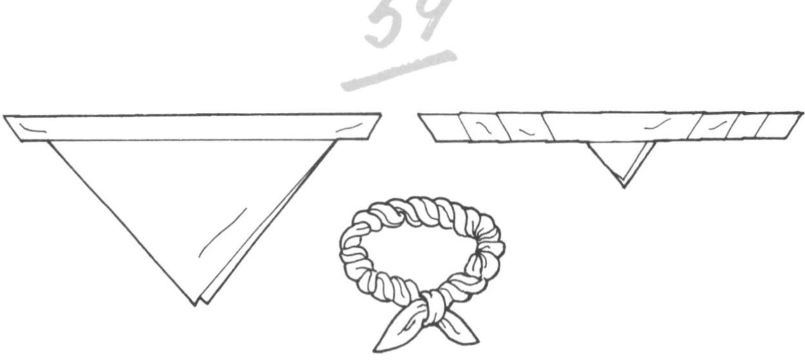

HEAD BAND

Fold a bandana into a triangle. Start with the folded edge, roll the bandana to a two inch width. Place the centre of the bandana on the forehead and tie a square knot at the back.

Variation

Fold a bandana on the bias and twist. Place the twisted bandana around the neck and tie a square knot.

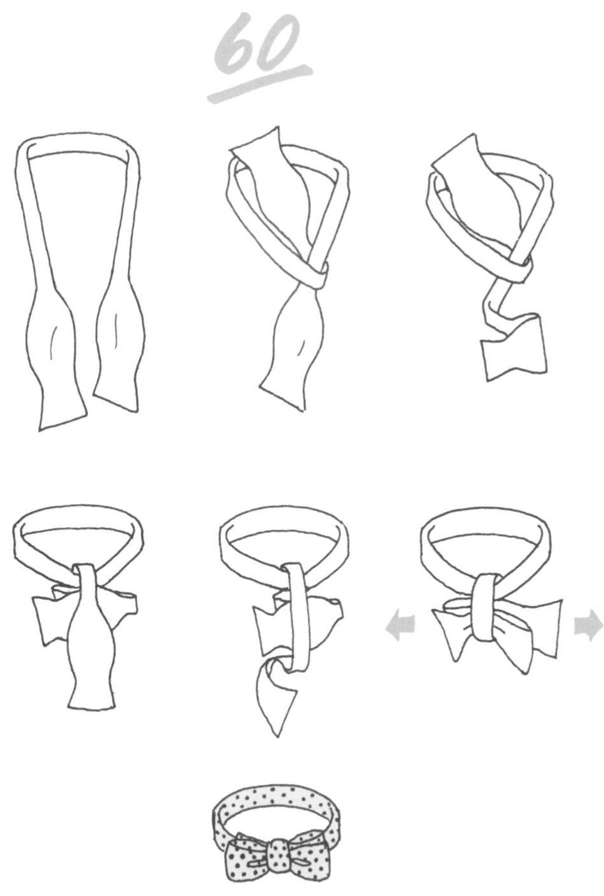

BOW TIE It's like tying your shoelace – only it's around your neck. Always use a mirror. Start by forming really small loops and you will be more successful in making your bow tie.

Place a tie or scarf around your neck. Keep one panel longer and cross the long panel over the top of the short panel and tie a single knot. Form a small half bow with the shorter panel. Hold in place with your thumb and forefinger. Let the longer panel fall over the half bow. Pinch the long panel just below the half bow and feed it in behind to form the second half of the bow. Balance the loops and ends together at the same time to even out the size of the traditional bow tie. Tighten the scarf by pulling the loops horizontally and spreading the bows. *"Now take a bow!"*

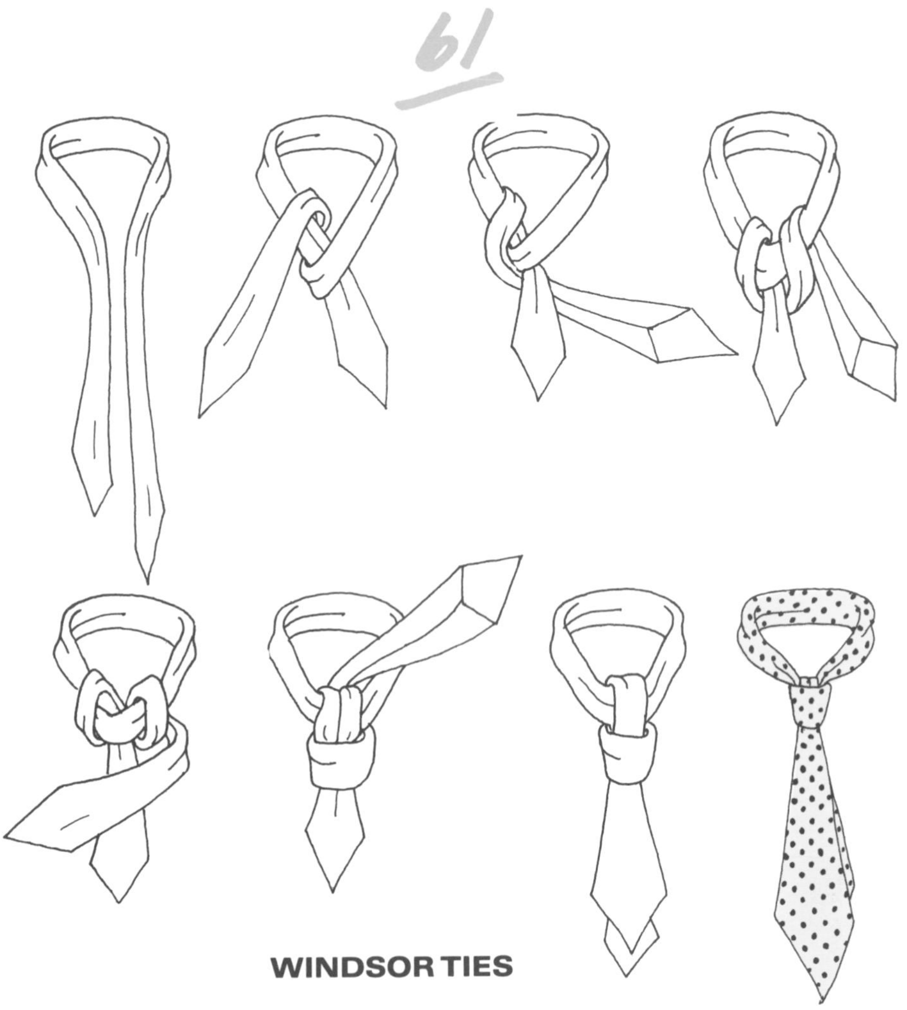

WINDSOR TIES

To tie a windsor knot it is important to begin with the wide panel much longer. Work only with the long panel. The short panel remains stationary.

THE FULL WINDSOR

The basis of the full windsor knot is done by looping the long panel around the neck band twice. This makes a balanced knot and gives a formal look.

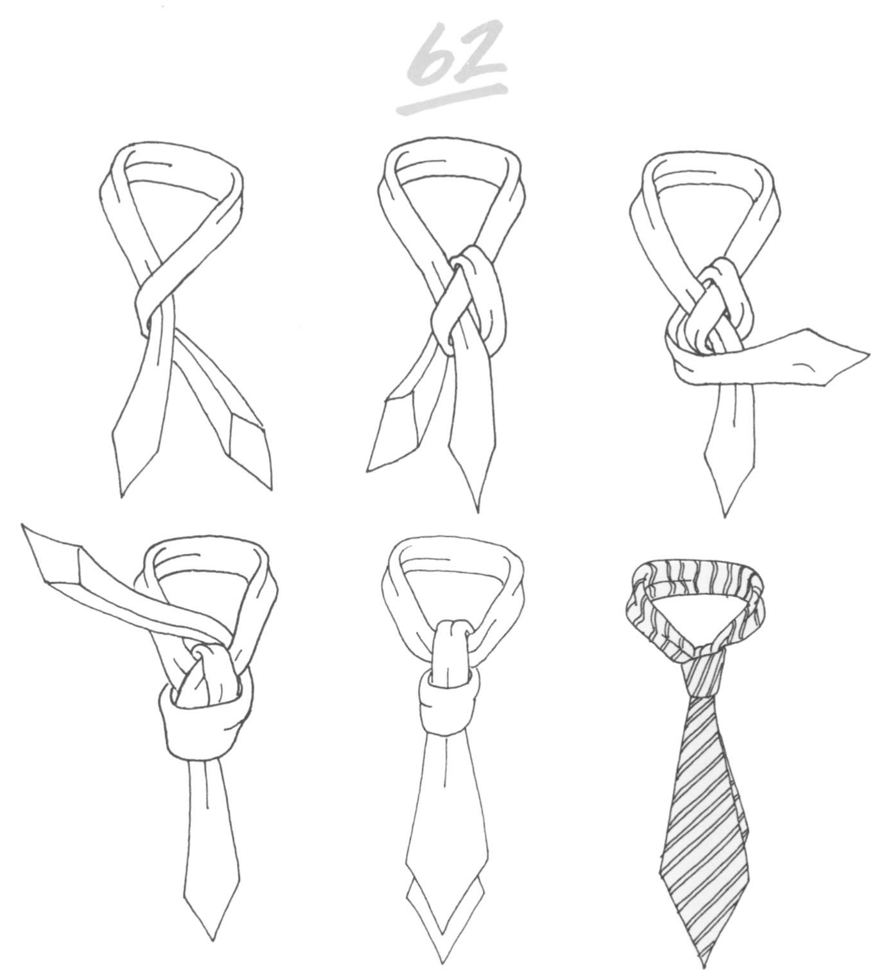

HALF WINDSOR

By looping the long panel around the neck band only once it creates a more casual finish with a slight angle to the knot.

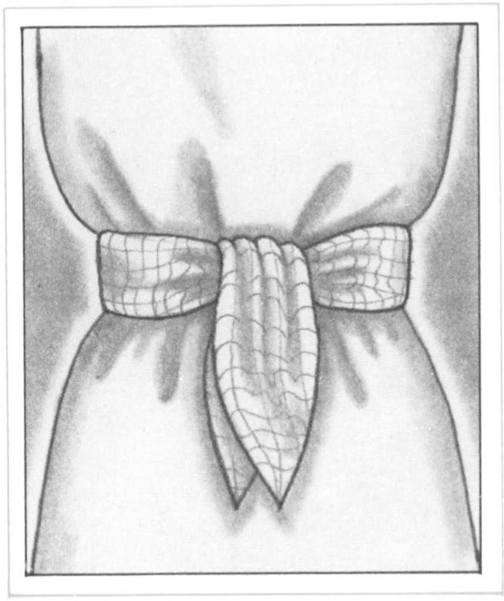

63

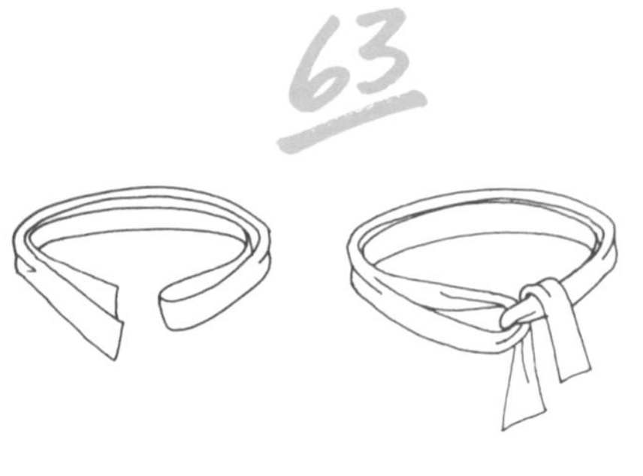

OVERLAP SASH

Fold a long narrow scarf or sash in half. Wrap it around the waist with the loop in front. Feed one panel through the loop from the top to the bottom and then the other panel through the loop from the bottom to the top. Tighten and smooth the panels.

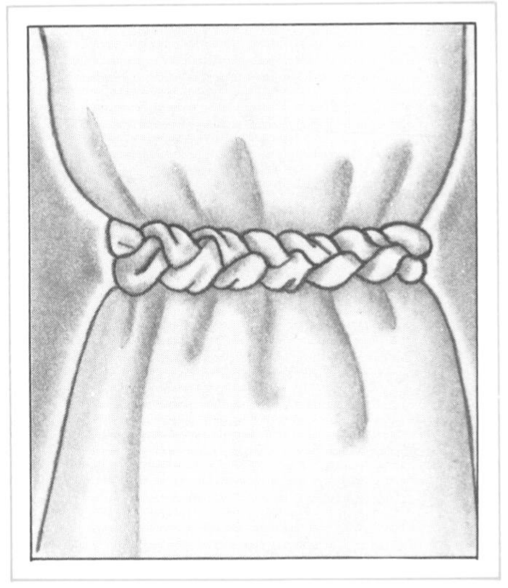

64

BRAIDED SASH

Place a long narrow scarf or sash around your waist. Tie a single knot over to one side keeping the ends even. Cross the bottom panel over the top panel and feed it up, under the waistband. Repeat with the other panel. Continue to braid and finish by tieing a square knot. Tuck the ends in or leave them to fall freely.

65

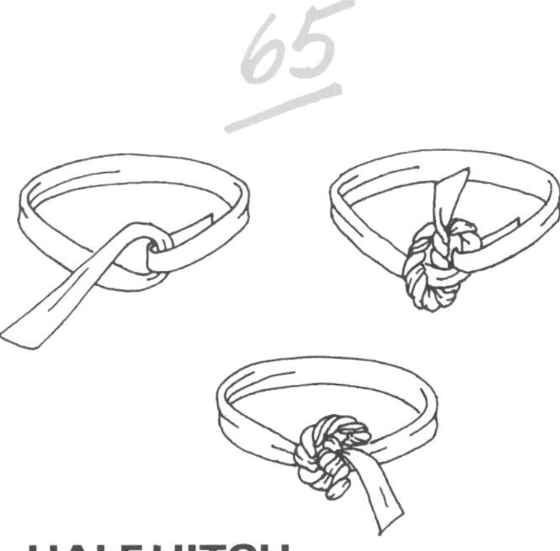

HALF HITCH

Use a long narrow, textured leather, scarf or sash. Fold under one end of a panel 8 inches (20 cm). Place the folded edge in the centre of your waist. Feed the long panel up through the loop and twist. Wrap the twisted panel around itself and feed under the waistband and up through the centre of the twisted loop. When using a lighter weight fabric, fold the sash or scarf in half first or tie a loop at one end.

66

DOUBLE WRAP TWIST

Place a long narrow scarf or sash at the front of your waist, bring the ends to the back, criss cross at the back and bring them forward. Tie a half bow, or a single knot and twist the panels together. Wrap the twisted panels around itself and tuck the ends into the centre of the twists. This will form a rosette.

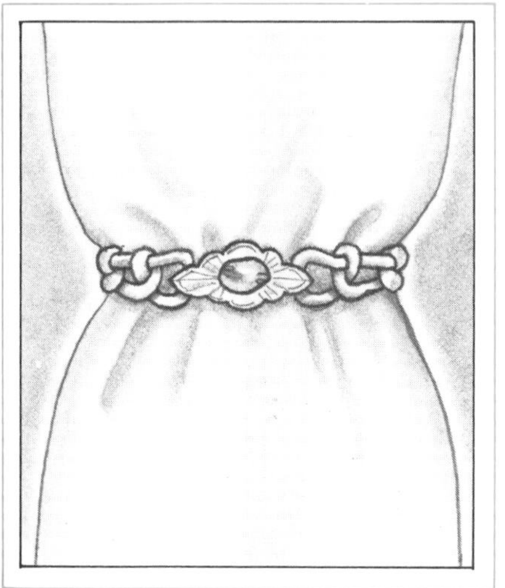

67

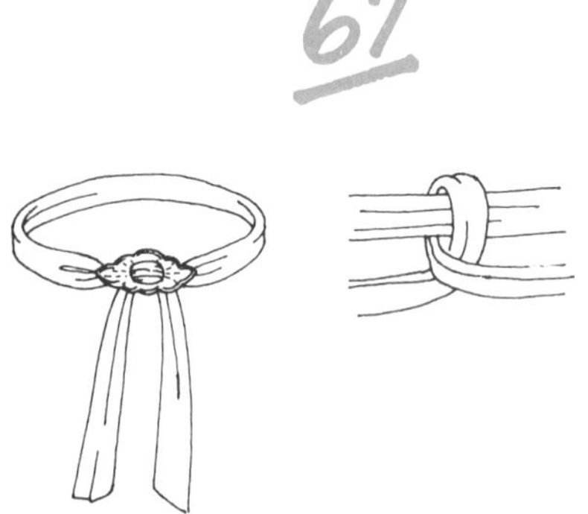

EASY CHAIN

Wrap a long narrow scarf or sash around the waist. Feed the ends through the openings of the accent from the back to the front. Tie a square knot and pass the ends back through the same openings keeping the panels even. With one panel at a time, feed the panel over top the waist-band, down behind and through the loop. Repeat and leave a space between, to the end of the panel. Tuck the end in. Repeat with other panel.

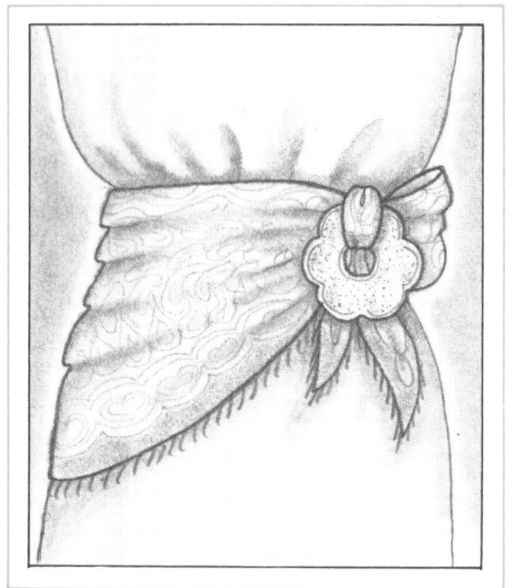

68

SHAWL HIP WRAP

Fold a large square scarf or shawl into a triangle. Place the triangle on one hip and tie a half bow and finish with the ends even. Feed the opening of the accent through the knot of the half bow. Pin into place. Spread the puff and the ends.

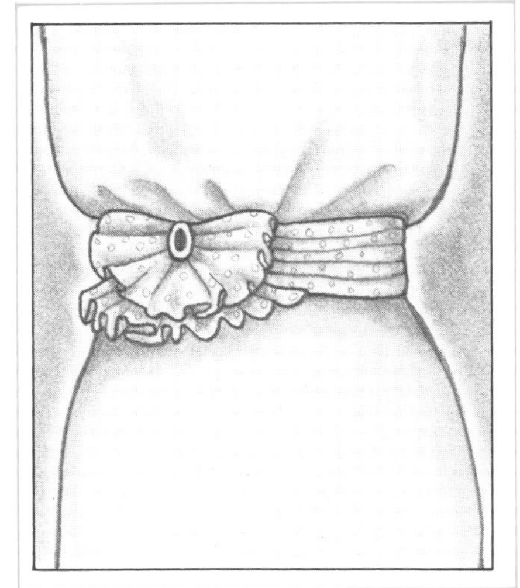

69

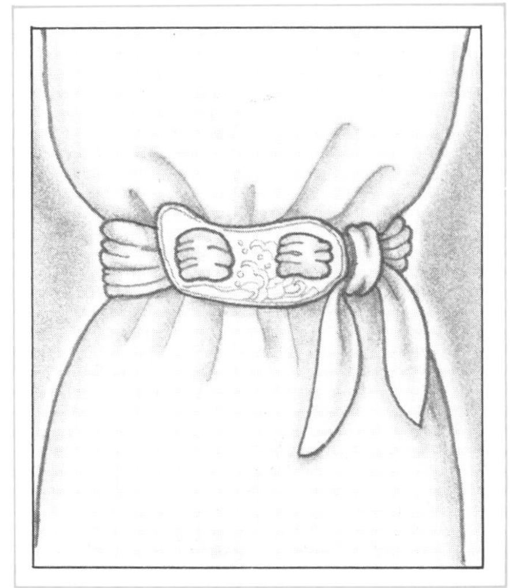

70

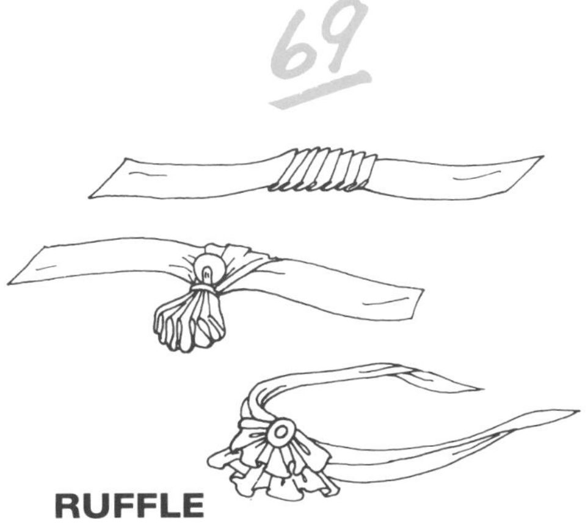

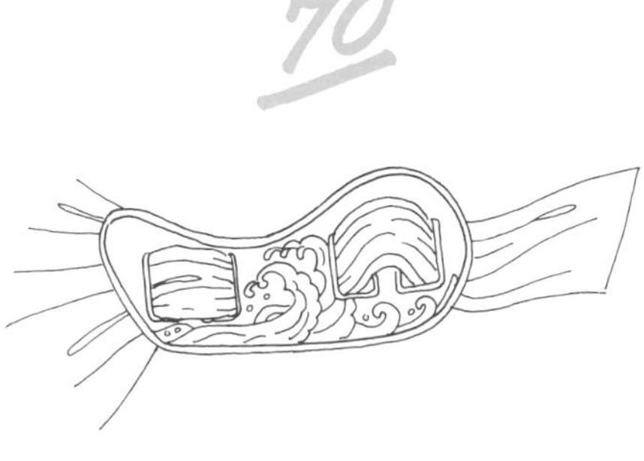

RUFFLE

Place an oblong or a bias scarf on a flat surface. With your fingers start to pleat about 15 inches from one end (35 cm) to the same distance from the other end. Holding the pleats in one hand, feed them down through the loop of the scarf clip to almost half way. Layer the pleats one on top of the other and close the clip. Take the ends to the back of your waist and tie a square knot.

SIDE KNOT

Weave a long narrow scarf or sash through the opening of the accent from the back to the front leaving one end longer. With the accent in front, wrap the long panel around your waist. Tie a square knot at the side of the accent.

MAIL ENQUIRIES TO:

HAMMETT ENTERPRISES
5250 Finch Ave. E., Unit 6
Scarborough, Ontario, Canada
M1S 5A4